THE OPTIMISTIC LIFE

OR,
In the Cheering-Up Business

By

ORISON SWETT MARDEN

AUTHOR OF
Pushing to the Front

First published in 1907

This edition published by Read Books Ltd.
Copyright © 2019 Read Books Ltd.
This book is copyright and may not be
reproduced or copied in any way without
the express permission of the publisher in writing

British Library Cataloguing-in-Publication Data
A catalogue record for this book is available
from the British Library

TABLE OF CONTENTS.

CHAPTER.		PAGE.
I.	IN THE CHEERING-UP BUSINESS	1
II.	THE POWER OF AMIABILITY	7
III.	YOUR HABITUAL EXPRESSION	16
IV.	THE INNER LIFE AS RELATED TO OUTWARD BEAUTY	18
	MAKING THE MOST OF A HAPPY TEMPER	20
V.	THE VALUE OF FRIENDS	23
VI.	COST OF AN EXPLOSIVE TEMPER	30
VII.	NON-ESSENTIALS	34
VIII.	MAKING A LIFE	37
IX.	LEARN TO EXPECT A GREAT DEAL OF LIFE	41
X.	MIND BUILDING	49
XI.	IF YOU CAN TALK WELL	59
XII.	BREVITY AND DIRECTNESS	65
XIII.	FROM AN EDITORIAL POINT OF VIEW	72
XIV.	THAT FEELING OF SMALLNESS	78
XV.	YOUR MOST VALUABLE POSSESSION	81
XVI.	SUPERIORITY THE BEST TRADE-MARK	88
XVII.	THE WATCHED BOY	96
XVIII.	THE RIGHT HAND OF GENIUS	100
XIX.	THE HONEY OF TOIL	109
XX.	UPON DISTINGUISHING WORK FROM DRUDGERY	117
XXI.	THE HABIT OF NOT FEELING WELL	122
XXII.	KEEPING FIT FOR WORK	132
XXIII.	THE POWDER OF SUCCESS	139
XXIV.	MASTERING MOODS	144

IN THE CHEERING-UP BUSINESS.

I.

IN THE CHEERING-UP BUSINESS.

WHEN Miss Edith Wyatt was at Bryn Mawr College, she was known as "the girl in the cheering-up business." Homesick girls, discouraged girls, girls who were behind in their studies, weary students went to her for a bit of brightness and encouragement, and always found it. She radiated mental sunshine from every pore.

There is a great opening in the cheering-up business, plenty of room for everybody, and it does not interfere with any other calling. One may do more good in it than in one's regular vocation.

Somehow these people have the power of unlocking the faculties, loosening the tongue, to make us speak with the gift of prophecy. These sunshine characters are health promoters. They are the unpaid boards of health who look after the public welfare.

The faculty of humor was given us to be developed as much as the faculty for earning a living. The universality of fun-loving shows its importance. It is as much our duty to develop the mirth-loving faculty as the mathematical faculty or language. There is every evidence that the fun-loving faculty was intended to be the strongest in human nature instead of the weakest. It ought to be developed and stimulated. It is the great medicine of the mind — the great uplifter and lubricator.

It is wonderful how the cultivation of the habit of enjoying things will transform the whole life, so that we see everything in a different light. This does not suggest frivolity or flippancy; it is the normal, natural development of humor, as it was exemplified in Beecher and in Phillips Brooks. Great healthy natures are always fun-loving.

It is positively sinful to suppress the mirthful tendencies in the young people — bubbling over, joyous and happy, exulting in mere existence. A serious and sober face on a child should be unthinkable. It is incompatible with God's plan. What has care and anxiety to do with young life? Care and anxiety and worry in a young face show that somebody is at fault.

"Laugh until I come back" was Father Taylor's good-bye to his friend Dr. Bartol. Yet many people have ruined their power of laughter. They have no rebound, no elasticity. To them the sense of humor is a weakness, frivolous and inconsistent with the dead-in-earnest, sober life. Life is a thing to be taken seriously, they say. These people feel the weight of the woes of the world. They are loaded down with this responsibility. They cannot understand how anybody can take such a light, flippant view of life as to spend time in fun-making. These people give us the impression that the whole universe would stop were it not for them. They go around with a serious aggrieved air with the world resting upon their shoulders.

Joyous people are not only the happiest, but the longest lived, the most useful and the most successful. This little strain of humor, the love of fun in human nature, is a normal, natural lubricant which oils life's machinery, makes it run smoothly, and relieves that jar and grinding of the bearings which prematurely wear away so many lives.

Lydia Maria Child used to say: "I think cheerfulness in every possible way. I hang prisms in my window to fill the room with rainbows." This is the right kind of philosophy, the great medicine of the mind, the best tonic for the body.

The habit of looking on the sunny side, the laughter-side or ludicrous side of things, is a fortune in itself. I would rather be a millionaire of cheerfulness and sunshine than of dollars.

No matter what your work may be, learn to find happiness everywhere. The love of cheerfulness can be cultivated like any other faculty — and in practical life it will be worth more to you than a college education without it. This is wealth that all can accumulate — the wealth of joy. No matter how hard your lot, how dark the day may seem, if you work a little good humor into it, it will lift your life above a humdrum existence. If you manage to get in a good laugh during the day, your work will not seem nearly as hard. It will relieve the grind and dreariness. A dull, serious mood all day will not only make you very uninteresting to others, but it makes your own load go hard. A good laugh does away with cares, worries, doubts, and relieves the great strain of modern life. If there is any one who bores us it is the man who has no fun in him, can never see a joke, who has no such sense of the ludicrous as to find something to excite laughter every hour of every day.

"Better a mind too small than one too serious." Give us the joy which is independent of circumstances, and which lifts us above even an iron environment.

> "Smile once in a while,
>   'T will make your heart seem lighter.
> Life's a mirror: if we smile,
>   Smiles come back to greet us;
> If we 're frowning all the while
>   Frowns forever meet us."

"You are on the shady side of seventy, I expect," some one said to an old gentleman. "No, I am on the sunny side of it."

In a country store in Connecticut men were discussing the question of how they would like to die. After the various preferences had been given, a man by the name of Zack was asked to give his preference. "Wal, I tell you, boys," he said, "I'd rather see something that would jest tickle me to death, and die a-laughin'."

An editor of a great daily was asked why he did not care for the services of a man past fifty. "It is not because he cannot do the work, but he takes himself too seriously."

In ancient Germany there was a law against joking. "It makes my men forget war," said the king. One would think that there was a law against laughter in our great cities, as he goes through the streets and sees among thousands scarcely a bright, cheerful face radiating sunshine. What a sad thing it is to go into the slums and see sad, sober, anxious looks upon the faces of many children, who ought to be all sunshine, radiating gladness. Joy has been crushed out of their little lives. Many of them never know what a glad childhood means.

One would think there had been an edict against laughter as he studies the faces of business and professional men in our cities. Even in restaurants or at lunch counters, men cannot forget the serious side of life. They eat with long faces. They are thinking, thinking, worrying, worrying, planning, planning. The almighty dollar is a serious subject, forbidding laughter during business hours.

Yet the pessimist repels trade and new business. The cheerful man attracts it. There is a great drawing power in optimism.

The hopeful man sees success where others see failure, sunshine where others see shadows and storm.

If the child were only brought up with the idea that the principal thing in life is to be cheerful under all circumstances it would soon revolutionize our civilization.

A great many people never learn to laugh heartily. A sort of a half smile is as far as they ever get. If children get a little boisterous they are hushed. Their little lives are suppressed in sad, serious homes until they almost lose the power of spontaneous laughter.

Dr. Johnson says: " A man should spend part of his time with the laughers." One of the redeeming features of the light plays and vaudeville performances is that people, temporarily at least, forget the serious side of life and learn to laugh.

How glad we all are to welcome a sunny soul. We are never too busy to see them. There is nothing we welcome so much as sunshine. It is a priceless gift to be able to possess a calm, serene, sweet soul which soothes, enriches, which is a perpetual balm to the hurts of the world. These souls reassure us. We seem to touch power and sympathy when they are with us, and we love to go near them when in trouble. They breathe a medicinal balm that soothes the wounds and hurts of the heart.

There is one success possible to the humblest man and the poorest woman; and that is, to go through life with a smiling face and to scatter the flowers of kindness on every hand. The habit of feeling kindly towards everybody, of carrying about a helpful manner, an expression of love, of kindness in one's very face, and a desire to help and cheer, is worth a fortune to a young man or young woman trying to get on. The wearer of smiles and the bearer of a kindly disposition needs no introduction, but is welcome everywhere.

There is nothing wanted so much in the world as sunshine, and the greatest wealth is a cheerful, helpful disposition. This is riches which not only blesses the possessor, but everybody he comes in contact with partakes of his wealth.

Everybody is rich who knows or comes in contact with the millionaire of good cheer, and the more he gives of his wealth, the more it multiplies. It is like the seed put into the soil — the more one sows, the greater the harvest.

"Do not look on life through a smoked glass."

II.

THE POWER OF AMIABILITY.

The noiseless sunbeam, the silent dewdrop, the unheard chemical processes in nature which are unfolding the germs of great future possibilities are infinitely more powerful and beneficial in their ultimate results than the tornado or the lightning.

The mightiest force in the world is the silent power of love.

The scolding woman, who is forever nagging and finding fault, has not a tithe of the power over man or in the home as the sweet-tempered, patient, amiable, loving one, for the latter transforms the brute forces in the entire family into sweet humanities.

One bad-tempered girl or woman has ruined not only the peace and comfort of many a home, but that of an entire neighborhood. If there is any pitiable person in the world it is the possessor of an uncontrolled temper. If a young man marries a girl with a bad temper he does n't know what he is bringing upon himself.

The woman of calm, sweet self-possession, who has perfect control of herself, no matter how plain in feature or form she may be, is infinitely more desirable for a wife than the most brainy and fascinating girl with an ugly temper.

Amiability means harmony in the home, in society,

everywhere; and harmony is health, is longevity, is happiness.

Every physician knows that irritability, an uncontrolled temper, not only shortens life, sometimes by many years, but soon becomes outlined upon the body.

Nothing seems more out of place or more incongruous than the presence of hard, ugly lines — temper wrinkles, — on a woman's face, where men look for the serene, the lovely, the divine.

A bad temper is a beauty-killer in which no woman can afford to indulge. It will soon transform the most charming face, making it ugly and repulsive. Sweetness and beauty will not long live with a bad temper. Some great physicians now assert that a single fit of temper has been known to take more than a year from a woman's life. Of course, the same argument is true of men, although the disastrous effects are much more noticeable in women, for we naturally look to them for beauty and amiability. A woman naturally prizes youth and beauty above almost everything else, and does not always realize that, every time she indulges in a fit of temper, or irritability, or fault-finding, or cutting sarcasm, she deepens the telltale lines around her mouth, and traces a little deeper the crow-tracks about her eyes, which will be perpetual reminders, long after her beauty has flown, of the cause of its departure.

Physiologists and physicians say that the sensitive face is the first to record any disturbance or irritation in the nervous system. Nerve energy is spent in every such indulgence in ill temper.

The eyes betray it in the loss of lustre. The flabby muscles show it. The telltale wrinkles reveal the internal conditions which cause them.

If there is one thing that a man prizes more than anything else it is the love of harmony, — physical and mental comfort. Permanent peace makes the ideal home for the average man, and a bad temper, which is likely to explode at the slightest irritation, is almost as dangerous to the safety of the household as the presence of gunpowder would be.

It seems unfortunate that the schools do not emphasize the power of amiability in producing harmony, health, longevity, happiness.

We all know remarkable people who have the wonderful faculty of turning the common water of life into the most delicious wine. Some people turn everything they touch into vinegar, others into honey. There is something in the mechanism of some minds which seems to transmute the most sombre hues into the most gorgeous tints.

Their very presence is a tonic, which invigorates the system and helps one to bear his burdens. Their very coming into the home seems like the coming of the sun after a long, dark, Arctic night. They seem to bring the whole system into harmony. Their smile acts upon one like magic, and dispels all the fog of gloom and despair. They seem to raise manhood and womanhood to a higher power. They unlock the tongue, and one speaks with a gift of prophecy. They are health promoters. They are death to dyspepsia, and increase the appetite.

Others have just the opposite effect. Their very presence depresses. One feels cold perspiration while in their company. Everything about them is chill and forbidding. They dry up thought. We cannot think or be natural when with them. Their sarcasm, irony, detractions, and pessimism repel, and one shrinks from them.

We knew a girl who, when she grew to full consciousness of her ugliness of body, her unattractiveness of person, resolved to make herself so beautiful in character, in manner, so cultivated in all that makes life worth living, that people would forget her physical handicaps. She had the most irregular features, a turned-up nose, was cross-eyed, had a very large mouth, a very unattractive figure and yet this lady has so completely overcome what most girls consider a fatal handicap that they would probably become morose, pessimistic, disagreeable, and drag out a most unhappy existence, that everybody who knows her loves her. Nobody looks at what she thought would be the great barrier to her popularity. By the cultivation of a gracious, sweet manner, by her patience and discipline she has so transformed herself that you utterly forget her plainness. The moment she speaks you are charmed, there is an inexplainable something about her manner which captivates you. It is more than a match for beauty, it's an expression of a kindly heart. She makes you feel that she has a real interest in you, that she sees a great many beautiful things in life which most people never notice. She makes you feel that she has a personal interest in what you do. She will question you about your ambition, what you long to do and to become. She captivates you by her gracious manner, her vivacious spirit, her evidences of a broadened mind and rare experience.

Here is a real beauty which is not evident for a few attractive years and then leaves one empty and unattractive. It will not fade with years; it is not ephemeral as mere physical beauty is, and is attainable to a large degree by the plainest girl. It is a beauty which you can carry with you into old age, or rather, it's a beauty which will drive away old age. For a sunny heart, a mind which is always cheerful and hopeful and sympathetic, age has little in common. No matter how plain you are, cultivate soul beauty, beauty that is more than skin deep. It's an expression of spirit which time cannot tarnish or erase. It's a beauty which enriches everybody that comes in contact with you.

We know an old lady who has always been extremely plain, and yet, although in her eighties, there is a marvelous lustre in her eyes, a sweet expression which captivates you every time she speaks. She was determined in her girlhood to compensate for her plainness. Her handicap was such a spur to her to redeem her very ugliness that she has succeeded in a marvelous degree, so that when at an age when physical beauty usually vanishes, she has attained a beauty which does not fade, a sweetness which is perennial, a loveliness which never leaves her face. A fine culture, serenity, dignity, repose speak in her face and look out of her manner. In fact, she has robbed old age of its ugliness and made it extremely attractive.

Oh, who can estimate the real wealth which inheres in a fine character, a life which flings out its exquisite perfume on every side, which brings joy and gladness into every home it enters, into every life it touches! These fine characters carry sunshine wherever they go. No gloom or discouragement can ever exist in their presence. Everything coarse and brutal flees before it as darkness and gloom flee before the rising sun. The greatest achievement possible to mortals is the sweetness in life which radiates from a fine and exquisite personality. How base and mean money and huge estates look in comparison! All other things fade before it. Its touch is like magic to win friendship, influence, and power.

The man who refuses to give, to share what he has received, is as foolish as the farmer who was so wrought upon by the conviction of a coming season of drought and the probable destruction of crops that he refused to plant his corn. He said that he would keep it in the crib, that he would not risk putting it into the ground lest it might rot and he be left without provisions for the winter. The drought did not come, however, and the result was that he went hungry, while his neighbors who had planted generously reaped an abundant harvest.

A great philanthropist said that he had saved only what he had given away, that the rest of his fortune seemed lost. What we give away has a wonderful power of doubling and quadrupling itself on the return bound. It is the greatest investment in the world. It comes back in geometrical progression. Give! give!! give!!! It is the only way to keep from drying up, from becoming like a sucked orange, — juiceless, insipid.

Selfishness is self-destruction. The man who never helps anybody, who tightly shuts his purse when there is a request to give, who says that all he can do is to attend to his own affairs, who never gives a thought to his neighbor, who hugs all his resources to himself, who wants to get all and give nothing in return, is the man who shrivels and dries up like the rosebud, who becomes small and mean and contemptible.

We all know those poor dwarfed souls who never give, who close the petals of their helpfulness, withhold the fragrance of their love and sympathy, and in the end lose all they tried to hoard for themselves. They are cold, lifeless, apathetic; all their sympathies have dried up; they cannot enter into the joys and sorrows, the higher and nobler emotions of human life. Their souls have been frozen by selfishness and greed. They have become so narrow and stingy that they fear to give even a kind word or smile lest they may rob themselves of something. They have rendered themselves incapable of radiating sunshine or happiness, and, by the working of an immutable law, they receive none.

A strong man, watching one who was delicate and undeveloped exercising in a gymnasium, said to him: "My dear young man, how foolish you are to waste your energy on those parallel bars and dumb-bells. You are weak, physically, and ought to save what strength you have for your day's work. You cannot afford to squander your vitality that way."

"Oh, but, my good sir," replied the other, "you don't see the philosophy underlying this exercise. The only way I can increase my power is by first giving out what I have. I give my strength to this apparatus, but it returns what I give it with compound interest. My muscles grow by giving it out in effort, in exercise."

Give and increase; hoard and lose! It is the universal law of growth.

"I will roll up my petals of beauty; I will withhold this precious fragrance, this love-incense of sun and dew for myself," said the selfish rosebud. "It is wasteful extravagance to give it away to careless passers-by." But, behold, the moment it tries to store up, to withhold its riches from others, they vanish! It shrivels and dies!

"I will give myself out," said the generous rose; "I will bestow my beauty and fragrance on everybody who passes my way," and, lo, it blossoms into a riot of sweetness and loveliness of which it never dreamed. It had only a tiny bit of fragrance until it tried to give that little to the world. Then, to its astonishment, it was flooded with sweet odors that came from somewhere,— evolved from the chemistry of the sunlight, the moisture in the air and the chemical forces in the soil.

The habit of doing good, of helping somebody every day, of dropping a little word of encouragement here and there, to a newsboy, a waiter in a restaurant or a hotel, a conductor on a car, an elevator boy, a toiler in your home or your office, a poor unfortunate man or woman in a wretched home, or on a seat in the park,— this is what broadens and ennobles life, makes character beautiful and fragrant as the rose; this is the sort of giving that returns to us with compound interest.

Everywhere we go we find opportunities for this sort of giving. Everywhere we find some one who needs encouragement, some one whose heart is breaking under a heavy load, some one who needs sympathy, some one who needs a lift. We never can tell what glorious fruitage the seed of the most trivial act of kindness may produce. Many a heart has been cheered simply by a smile from a stranger. A look of sympathy, an expression of a desire to help, a warm grasp of the hand has brought back hope and courage to many a disheartened soul. A kind letter, a word of encouragement has been the turning-point in the career of many a person on the verge of despair.

There are gifts more precious than anything money can buy, which are in the power of all to bestow. The little girl who spent all her pennies in buying paper and a postage stamp to write to her grandmother at Christmas and say, "I love you, I love you, dear grandmamma," teaches us a splendid lesson.

Give, give, give, of whatever you have; but give yourself with your gift. It is love for which the world is hungering. "Scatter your flowers as you go, for you will not pass this way again."

III.

YOUR HABITUAL EXPRESSION.

WHAT kind of an expression do you wear habitually? Is it sour, morose, repellant? Is it a mean, stingy, contemptible, uncharitable, intolerant expression? Do you wear the expression of a bulldog, a grasping, greedy, hungry expression, which indicates an avaricious nature? Do you go about among your employees with a thundercloud expression, with a melancholy, despondent, hopeless look on your face, or do you wear the sunshine expression, which radiates a feeling of good will and of helpfulness? Do people smile and look happier when you approach them, or do they shrink from you, and feel a chilly goose-flesh sensation come over them as they see you approach?

It makes all the difference in the world to you and to those whom you influence what kind of an expression you wear.

I once worked for a man who had a habitual smile which was worth a fortune to him. No matter how angry he might be inside, you never could tell it by his face. There might be a volcano just ready to break out, yet his face would wear that serene, happy, contented smile. One corner of his mouth always curved up as though he had received some good news and was just dying to tell you about it.

A great many people wondered at his success. They thought it far outreached his ability; but there is no doubt that a great deal of it was due to that inimitable smile which never left him. It made hosts of friends for him and brought many customers to his store.

There is power in a habitual smile, not only because it wins friends and brings customers, but its influence over one's own life is immeasurable. The effort to be always cheerful, kind, considerate, and gentle, no matter what wars may be rankling in the heart, has a great influence in transforming the life.

I know a lady who has made it a habit of her life to diffuse sunshine everywhere she goes. She says that a smile costs nothing. The result is that everybody who waits upon her or does anything for her feels it a real favor to serve her, because he is always sure of getting this indescribably sweet smile and expression in return.

What a satisfaction it is to go through life giving out life and hope instead of despair, encouragement instead of discouragement, and to feel conscious that even the newsboy or the bootblack, the car conductor, the office boy, the elevator boy, or anybody else with whom one comes in contact, gets a little dash of sunshine. It costs nothing when you buy a paper of a boy, or get your shoes shined, or pass into an elevator, or give your fare to a conductor, to give a smile with it, to make these people feel that you have a warm heart and good will. Such salutations will mean more to us than many of the so-called great things. It is the small change of life. Give it out freely. The more you give, the richer you will grow.

IV.

THE INNER LIFE AS RELATED TO OUTWARD BEAUTY.

WE once knew a little girl who said that she "was so happy because everybody loved her so." She could not see how anybody could be unhappy. Everybody loved her because she loved them. She would go out in the fields and clap her hands for the very joy of being alive. Every bird and flower and shrub seemed to say to her, "Be happy."

But why should we not all feel this way? Everybody and every object of nature is an expression of some Divine idea, and if we see things through the eyes of innocence and truth, if we see things as God made them, and not the distorted images which we see through the ugly glasses of our own wrong thinking and vicious living, if we could see realities, everything would say to us, "Be happy, be successful; be harmonious." If we were perfectly normal, we should be so contented and happy that life would be a perpetual joy. There will be no poverty, no suffering when all the world arrives at the point where everybody can see realities and live the truth.

It always seems incongruous to see a hard, greedy, grasping, selfish face in the country. It is so out of keeping with all the suggestive beauty and symbolisms of God. Such discord has no place in God's harmony. What a contrast between such a face and the loveliness and sweetness which are radiated from flowers and meadows, forest and birds.

A stranger who saw such a face in the midst of natural grandeur and beauty would say that it must have dropped to the earth from some other planet; that it could never have been developed on this beautiful earth.

Selfishness and greed and sin, and all discordant conditions, have no place in God's kingdom. They are foreign to all that He has made. The only wrong things in the universe come from wrong thinking, vicious living.

Only the "pure in heart" can "see God" or good; only the transparent, sinless mind can see realities, can see beauties. Every sinful thought and every wrong thought, every vicious act hangs an additional film over the eye that sees the things as God made them; and we must get these films off by right thinking and right living before we can see the world as God made it or appreciate the man as God made him.

Every film of selfishness or self-seeking, every film of dishonesty or taking advantage of another, of standing in another's way or keeping another back, must be removed before we can get the clear, crystalline vision of reality, of truth.

Many of us keep adding these films in our efforts to get pleasure and profit, until our spiritual vision is completely lost, until the lens of our vision becomes absolutely opaque and we can see nothing but the gross, the material. Everything looks black and sordid through the selfish, greedy, dishonest glasses.

No man can see anything in this world except through the lens of his own acts, of his own thought, of his own motives. The vision must be colored by the medium through which we look. Every act of our lives, every thought, every motive is hung up before our eyes, and we are compelled to look at everything through them. If the act is clean, the thought is pure, and the deed is true, there will be perfect transparency, and we shall see truth and beauty and realities instead of distorted, ugly, vicious, hideous images. We must get the films off the eyes before we can get perfect vision.

MAKING THE MOST OF A HAPPY TEMPERAMENT.

When God made the rose He said :. " Thou shall flourish and spread thy perfume." This is the command that came to us when we came out of the silence into this world : " Scatter thy perfume, thy flowers, thy sunshine as thou goest along, for thou wilt never go over the same road again."

Did you ever realize how many friends and business patrons you may drive away through a habitual sour, repulsive expression and a repellant manner? Everybody is trying to get out of the gloom into the light, out of the cold into the warmth. Everybody is looking for brightness, trying to get away from shadows into the sunshine. They want to get into harmony and away from discord.

The art of optimism, if understood and practised, would change the face of the world. Just try the cultivation of the sunny side of your nature for a year. It would revolutionize your whole life. You would attract where now you repel; warm and cheer where now, perhaps, you chill and discourage. Compare the power of a shadow with that of a ray of sunlight. All the life, all the physical force on the globe is in the stored up energy of the sunbeam. There is no life or hope in the darkness. How we love people who always carry sunshine; we look at them to get new inspiration and renew our confidence in human nature. We turn to them naturally, as the sunflower turns its face to the sun; and we turn as naturally away from the faces that are overcast, — where a thunderstorm seems to be gathering. The bright, joyous heart is a great boon, and the face that carries habitual sunshine is a perpetual blessing.

We make the world we live in and shape our own environment. Some of us live in dungeons of our own making, then complain of the darkness and the gloom. The pessimists, the men and women who see darkness, despair, disaster and deterioration everywhere, the people who see the world going backwards, carry very little weight compared with the optimists, the men and women who see the best in everything, who see the man and the woman that God made, not those that disease and discord and sin have marred and scarred. It is the men that see the world that God made with all its beauty, its sunshine and promise and hope, not the people who see the ugliness, the deformity everywhere, who have lifted civilization up from barbarity to its present condition. These benignant faces which scatter serenity and hope do more to lift the burdens of the world than the thousand long-faced, sober people who tell you to prepare for the world to come, but never have a smile for the world they are in.

The qualities we cultivate will finally dominate the thought, will outpicture themselves on the body, and will rule the life. We find that the world we live in is the one that is reflected from within us. The world flings us back the echoes of our own voices, our own thoughts.

If we are sad and gloomy it will fling back despair, discouragement and hopelessness; but if we turn to it a sunny face and a bright, satisfied heart it will give us back the same in kind.

One person finds enjoyment wherever he goes, everything seems to suggest pleasure and happiness to him, he finds everybody kind and accommodating, everybody seems glad to aid him and favor him or show him a courtesy; another frets and complains and finds fault at everything, sees no cause for joy, and looks upon the world as a cold, dismal, forbidding place,— and he finds just what he is looking for.

The whole world is but a whispering gallery, an echoing hall, which flings back the echo of our own complaints or commendations; a mirror which reflects the face we make in it.

V.

THE VALUE OF FRIENDS.

"Friends are each other's mirrors, and should be clearer than crystal or the mountain springs, and free from clouds, design, or flattery."

"LINCOLN has nothing only plenty of friends," was often said of the young Illinois lawyer. Poor in purse as he was, he was rich in his friendships, and he rose largely by their aid. "Win hearts, and you have hands and purses," said Lord Burleigh, cynically phrasing a great social principle.

No young man starting in life could have better capital than plenty of friends. They will strengthen his credit, support him in every great effort, and make him what, unaided, he could never be. Friends of the right sort will help him more — to be happy and successful than much money or great learning.

When Garfield entered Williams College he won the friendship of its president, Mark Hopkins. Years afterwards, when President of the United States, he said: "If I could be taken back into boyhood to-day, and have all the libraries and apparatus of a university with ordinary routine professors offered me on the one hand, and on the other a great, luminous, rich-souled man, such as Dr. Hopkins was twenty years ago, in a tent in the woods alone, I should say, 'Give me Dr. Hopkins for my college course, rather than any university with only routine professors.'"

Charles James Fox, unfortunate in his home training, had many defects remedied through association with Edmund Burke.

History, both sacred and profane, is full of examples of the effects of friendship on character.

"What is the secret of your life?" asked Elizabeth Barrett Browning of Charles Kingsley; "Tell me that I may make mine beautiful, too." "I had a friend," was the reply. This is the secret of great and successful lives. Many a man would have lain down disheartened, long before he reached his goal, but for the stimulus and encouragement of some friend whose name the world has never heard. Hundreds who are lauded in the press, and honored all over the world for their achievements, owe their success largely to the encouragement of wives, mothers, sisters, or other intimate friends.

The average man little realizes how great a part even of his material success he owes to his friends; he takes to himself the entire credit of every achievement, boasting of his own marvelous insight, judgment, and hard work. If, however, we should take out of our lives everything contributed, directly or indirectly, by friends, — if we should eliminate the inspiration and practical helpfulness they have given us, — if we should deduct from our popularity the percentage due to their good words, and give up situations they helped us to gain, the majority of us would find a great shrinkage in what we thought our own achievement.

A young lawyer starting in practice often has plenty of time to cultivate friends, and that is the wisest thing he can do — every one who knows him is trying to help him to success. His friends tell others that he will be

JAMES ABRAM GARFIELD.

THE VALUE OF FRIENDS. 25

sure to make his mark, that they would not be surprised to see him in the legislature, in Congress, or, perhaps, on the supreme court bench. No matter how able or how brilliant he may be, or how well versed in the niceties of the law, very few will be willing to intrust cases to an inexperienced young man if he is not supported by this mouth to mouth recommendation of friends.

It is the same with a young physician trying to get a start. All his friends are anxious to lend him a helping hand. They know how difficult it is for one untried, even if thoroughly prepared, to establish sufficient confidence in his skill to induce people to trust him with patients in preference to experienced practitioners. They praise his skill; they tell how sick they were and how quickly he aided them. In a short time the whole neighborhood begins to look favorably on him and, of course, he gets patients.

The case of a young merchant beginning with small capital differs only in kind from that of an author, lawyer, or physician. No matter how honest he may be or how square in his dealings, he is unknown and untried. He has to win his way to the favor of the general public. The business maxim, "A pleased customer is the best advertisement," is a tribute to the commercial value of friends, — for one must feel friendly to recommend a store and its goods.

The service, however, that friends render in advancing our material interests is the lowest standpoint from which friendship can be viewed. To choose our friends with an eye to their commercial value to us would be to proclaim ourselves unworthy of the friendship of any noble soul, and indeed incapable of winning any friendship worthy of the name.

It is in relation to their effect on character that the value of friends must be estimated. Dr. Hillis says that "Destiny is determined by friendship; fortune is made or marred when a youth neglects his companions." Character is tinted by the friends to which we attach ourselves. We borrow their color, black or white. We absorb their qualities, whether they be noble or ignoble. "Men become false," says Charles Kingsley, "if they live with liars; cynics, if they live with scorners; mean, if they live with the covetous; affected, if they live with the affected; and actually catch the expressions of each other's faces."

Beecher said he was never quite the same man again after he had read Ruskin's works. Our best friends often are authors in their books. No one is quite the same again who has been touched by a noble friendship and has felt the expression of a lofty mind stirring the divinity within him and giving him a glimpse of his real self.. Such friends we often gain through reading.

Some people act like a tonic or an invigorating and refreshing breeze. They make us feel like new beings. Under the inspiration of their presence we can say and do things which it would be impossible for us to say and do under different conditions. One stimulates my thought, quickens my faculties, sharpens my intellect, opens the floodgates of language and sentiment, and awakens the poetic within me. While another dampens my enthusiasm, closes the door of expansion, and chills me to the very centre of my being, there emanates from him an atmosphere which paralyzes thought, dwarfs expression.

CHARLES KINGSLEY.

"Our chief want in life," says Emerson, "is somebody who shall make us do what we can. This is the service of a friend. With him we are easily great. There is a sublime attraction in him to whatever virtue there is in us. How he flings wide open the door of existence! What questions we ask of him! What an understanding we have! How few words are needed! It is the only real society. A real friend doubles my possibilities, adds his strength to mine, and makes a well-nigh irresistible force possible to me."

The example or encouragement of a friend has proved the turning-point in many a life. How many dull boys and girls have been saved from failure and unhappiness by discerning teachers or friends who saw in them possibilities that no one else could see, and of which they were themselves unconscious! Those who appreciate us, who help to build up instead of destroying our self-confidence, double our power of accomplishment. In their presence we feel strong and equal to almost any task that may confront us.

Many people living to-day almost worship the memory of Phillips Brooks. Filled with an intense belief in man's possibilities, he aroused many a mediocre youth to a realization of the strength that lay dormant within him, made him feel almost a giant, and inspired him to do things of which he would not otherwise have believed himself capable. He made those who came in contact with him feel that it was mean and contemptible to look down when they could look up, to grovel when they could soar, or to do the lower when the higher was possible.

Ah, there is no other stimulator, helpmeet, or joy-giver like a true friend! Well might Cicero say: "They seem to take away the sun from the world who withdraw friendship from life; for we have received nothing better from the immortal gods, nothing more delightful."

Friendship is no one-sided affair, but an exchange of soul qualities. There can be no friendship without reciprocity. One cannot receive all and give nothing, or give all and receive nothing, and expect to experience the joy and fulness of true companionship.

Those who would make friends must cultivate the qualities which are admired and which attract. If you are mean, stingy, and selfish, nobody will admire you. You must cultivate generosity and large-heartedness; you must be magnanimous and tolerant; you must have positive qualities, for a negative, shrinking, apologizing roundabout man is despised. You must cultivate courage and boldness, for a coward has few friends. You must believe in yourself. If you do not, others will not believe in you. You must look upward and be hopeful, cheery, and optimistic. No one will be attracted to a gloomy pessimist.

The moment a man feels that you have a real live interest in his welfare, and that you do not ask about his business, profession, book, or article merely out of courtesy, you will get his attention, and will interest him. You will tie him to you just in proportion to the intensity and unselfishness of your interest in him. But if you are selfish, and think of nothing but your own advancement; if you are wondering how you can use everybody to help you along; if you look upon every man or woman you are introduced to as so much more possible success-capital; if you measure people by the amount of business they can send you, or the number of new clients, patients, or readers of your book they can secure for you, they will look upon you in the same way. If you have friends don't be afraid to express your friendship; don't be afraid to tell them that you admire or love them. If you love anybody, why not say so? If you enjoy any one's company, why not say so? It costs you nothing; it may mean everything to your friend, and to your friendship.

A lady was asked how she managed to get along so well with disagreeable people. "It is very simple," she replied; "all I do is to try to make the most of their good qualities and pay no attention to their disagreeable ones." No better formula by which to win and hold friends could be found.

A man should start out in life with the determination to never sacrifice his friendships. He must keep them alive or sacrifice a part of his manhood and a part of his success. There must be a live wire kept continually between him and them.

"Those friends thou hast, and their adoption tried, grapple them to thy soul with hooks of steel;" and, as old friends are removed by death or other causes, do not fail to replace them. You cannot afford to narrow the circle of your friends, for the measure of your success and happiness and your usefulness will be largely proportioned to the number and quality of your friends.

VI.

THE COST OF AN EXPLOSIVE TEMPER.

MANY men and women are jogging along in mediocrity, occupying inferior places because they are unable to keep good situations on account of hot tempers. Everywhere we see people mortified, humiliated, kept down by hot tempers which they think they cannot control. They may work months or years to climb up to good positions and throw them away by yielding to fits of passion in moments of annoyance.

I have in mind a man who spent twenty years preparing himself for a responsible position, one which would have meant a competence to himself and family for life, and lost it in five minutes in a paroxysm of passion. He could not control himself.

I know a man who has letters of endorsement from great men of position and power, a man who has been in important positions himself, but has never been able to keep one of them any length of time. He has lots of energy, a great deal of perseverance, and every time he is knocked down he gets up and starts again, but is n't it pitiable to see a gray-haired man with a family, a man of great ability, perpetually humiliated by being thrown out of positions? Is n't it sad to see an able man, with a vigorous brain, full of energy and life, go around asking help of his friends to get clothing, food and shelter for his family, simply because of a hot temper?

I met a very capable man the other day who has been handicapped all his life by a quick temper, which is the secret of his comparative failure. He has held many good positions but lost them in unguarded moments. He is very ambitious and hardworking, and he struggles to get ahead. He is now well along in years, but he has never been able to do anything such as which his superior ability would warrant. He feels mortified every time I meet him that he is filling such an ordinary position when he is perfectly conscious that he has superior ability. He knows that he ought to be at the top of his profession instead of half way down; that he ought to be a leader instead of being led by men who are not half so competent as he. It galls him to death to be ordered around by men far his inferior in ability, but they all know his fault, which, so far as his getting on in the world is concerned, is almost as bad as drunkenness itself, for he has been the slave of a hot temper.

Can anything be more foolish than for a boy to spend years and years on an education and special training for his lifework and then just as soon as he climbs up a little and gets a decent position, to throw it all away in a momentary fit of temper? What would you think of an artist who would spend years in calling a beautiful statue out of a marble block and then smite it to pieces with his mallet in an instant, then go to work on another and do the same thing again and again? You would say that he ought to be in an insane asylum. But are you sure, my friend, that you are not even more foolish than he; that you are not destroying your own work of years by hasty explosions of temper?

People who fly into rage at the slightest criticism, who take everything as a personal affront, are never sure of themselves, never sure of their positions. They make employers and associates feel all the time as if they were walking on thin ice, liable any minute to go through. You have to be very careful how you handle these touchy people, how you approach them; you always have to choose the right word lest you give offence. You must not say anything which they can twist into a personal thrust. These sensitive souls suffer a great deal, and they are very disagreeable people to get along with. Sensitiveness is really an acknowledgment of weakness. It is founded on vanity, false pride, egotism and selfishness.

One of the most difficult persons for an employer to manage is a girl who has been tenderly reared, who is high-strung and sensitive of the humiliation in having to work for a living. She is all the time being imposed upon, insulted. Her sore spots are always lacerated and they bleed at the slightest touch, intentional or unintentional. In fact, the greatest part of the suffering of a sensitive person is not intentionally inflicted and would not hurt any one else.

The man in high position who gets red in the face and flies off on a tangent every few minutes, at very little provocation, cuts no large figure. Everybody laughs at him and pities him for his weakness. To go through life making a fool of one's self several times every day by exhibiting one's foolish, weak, silly side, holding up to the ridicule of the world one's wishy-washy character is most unfortunate. It is not the part of a man, but that of a pigmy, a mere apology for a man, not the man God made.

Can anything be more humiliating than to feel that you do not really belong to yourself, to feel that you are

THE COST OF AN EXPLOSIVE TEMPER. 33

liable, no matter how good your intention, or how hard you work, to undo in a moment all you have done? You ought to be surer of yourself than that. You ought not only to think, but also to know positively that you can master yourself under all circumstances; and until you can do this you will never get very far up.

Now, when you think of being able to manage a bad temper, it seems a formidable task, almost impossible; but when you analyze the temper, you will find that it is made up of elements which you can control, and if you can control the elements' you can control the temper itself. Jealousy enters into a quick temper. So does intolerance of others' opinions. The victim wants to run things, wants to make everybody do as he wishes, and if he cannot he "flies off the handle." As a rule, a hot-tempered person is naturally arbitrary, selfish, envious, vain, proud. He cannot think of anybody else but himself. Other people's rights cut very little figure with him.

Every person should be ambitious to become a power in the world, to stand for something above the ordinary, to lift himself out of mediocrity; but he can never make himself thus felt until he is first master of himself. He cannot control conditions or men until he can first control himself. It is the man who can wait, no matter how trying it is, who can be calm no matter what the provocation, who can keep his balance under any circumstances, who can look serene when the tempest of passion is raging all around him in others, who is never thrown off his centre, — he it is who inspires confidence, who forces respect, and who masters men and matters.

VII.

NON-ESSENTIALS.

WE know people who have wasted a good part of their lives on non-essentials. They are always doing things which amount to nothing. We know women who are always looking for trouble, who are upset at fingermarks on the furniture, china or glassware, and who destroy the peace of the whole household because the cook has burned the soup or spoiled the pudding. They make the servants' lives miserable by nagging them about trifling neglects.

If you want to make the most of life you must make up your mind to overlook a great many things, — not to see them at all so far as being troubled by them is concerned. Never allow yourself to be upset because the cook has spoiled some favorite dish. Do not ruin the visit of your guests or embarrass the waitress by scolding her at the table because of some little mistake.

How many mothers we know who keep the whole household irritated over non-essentials. Some trifling thing sets them going, and they keep up their scolding and nagging and fault-finding until everybody in the house is disgusted.

These are not things that make life worth living. Learn to let go the rubbish, to throw overboard the useless cargo which endangers the safety of the ship.

Learn to let go everything which irritates, but does not help.

A great many people are like pins in the clothing, which prick us constantly, but which we cannot get rid of. A great many teachers really spoil the comfort and happiness of their pupils by exaggerating the importance of non-essentials. This is a most unfortunate habit of a great many people — the temptation to exaggerate trifles, to make mountains out of mole hills, to keep arguing and talking over a little thing until it becomes a big thing and destroys everybody's peace.

People who exaggerate non-essentials are like gravel in the shoe. You cannot stop in the street to take it out, and yet it destroys all your comfort of walking.

A great many business men keep the people about them irritated all the time by exaggerating things which do not amount to anything. If a stenographer makes a mistake they make her life miserable for hours, — perhaps days. Life is too short for quibbling over things which are not worth while.

We know people who waste half of their energies and make themselves extremely uncomfortable over little, insignificant non-essentials.

We have no energy to throw away. We must use every bit of it in the things that count if we would make the most of life. Many people are like a boiler full of holes, wasting a large part of the steam which should drive the piston and turn the wheel. Their force is frittered away in useless things that help nobody, and only hinder.

How many girls and young women form this wretched habit of spending time over things which do not count, wasting their energies over a particular shade of ribbon, or the proper thing in a hat, or a glove that is the fad. It is very important and very essential that they should exercise good taste in the selection of everything. We do not mean this at all. It is the waste of precious time over the things which do not count in life, which are not worth while, that we deprecate. It is a most unfortunate habit to contract of wasting one's life over the things which are not worth while to the neglect of things which are.

We have known women to wear themselves out hunting for a trifling thing in the stores — to spend half a day, perhaps, in fruitless search for some trifling matter of dress which amounted to nothing. It is pitiable to see such a waste of precious time and energy when this time spent in self-improvement, in self-culture, or helping somebody, or doing something worth while, would count for so much. This frittering away energies, squandering time over useless trifles, is positively wicked.

We have seen business men in restaurants disgust everybody within their hearing by their outburst of temper because the waiter did not happen to bring them the particular thing they called for, because the steak was rare when they wanted it well done, because he brought pudding for a pie, or boiled potatoes instead of baked, or because he happened to drop a little soup on their coat.

Sometimes we have known mothers to upset the whole household and destroy the comfort of everybody at dinner because the husband or one of the children happened to be late. These exacting people who run everything by programme — everybody must be on time to the very minute or take an unmerciful scolding — **make** life miserable for everybody around them.

VIII.

MAKING A LIFE.

THERE is something better than putting money into the pocket. Put beauty into the life.

Do not focus the energies of a lifetime upon money making. Rich men hug their gold; and yet their possibilities of beauty and grandeur of character have never been developed — the priceless pearl for which they have sold all else.

But what does all this life struggle mean if the beautiful side, the tender side, the affectionate side is never to be developed? Is there nothing better than the sordid scramble for money, for place? Is selfishness, personal aggrandizement, the greatest thing in life? Is there nothing finer and dearer and more beautiful to struggle for?

One would think to go through one of our great cities, ward after ward, one barren area after another, that there is but one thing to struggle for, — the material; that the beautiful has little place. Everything suggests the material: plain, square, homely buildings of all heights, sizes, dimensions, with little idea of symmetry, of the æsthetic; bridges, approaches to parks, squares, and cities are plain and ugly to an extreme. Everything must give way to the god, the "useful." Were the inhabitants of Paris transferred to New York or

Chicago they would have a perpetual headache. Their sense of the beautiful would be shocked. Most American homes are ugly in the extreme. Instead of keeping in mind the graceful, the beautiful, the artistic, everywhere it is the everlasting useful — the square, the angular, the repulsive. Instead of the graceful curve, the beautiful arched effect, the Gothic, both dwelling rooms and assembly rooms are built on the plan of the dry goods box. Are we not too severe, too hard, too practical?

Are we never to rank refined culture as superior to the sordid money-getting faculties? Are we forever to devote ourselves to the coarse side of man, while the God-side, the intellectual, the moral remains undeveloped? Who can estimate the real wealth that inheres in a fine character and a cultivated life, which brings joy and gladness into every home it enters, into every street car, store, factory, or office, — wherever it goes. It was said that the soldiers in hospitals in the Crimean War used to say they could feel when Florence Nightingale was coming, long before they could see her. They could feel her refined personality, her sweet influence radiating everywhere. These fine characters carry sunshine and gladness wherever they go. No gloom or discouragement can exist in their presence. Everything coarse and brutal flees before them as darkness and gloom flee before the rising sun. The greatest achievement possible to mortals is the cultivation of the sweetness and light which radiate from a refined and exquisite personality. How base and mean money and huge estates look in comparison. All other things fade before it. Its touch is like magic to win friendship, influence, power. Can you afford to chill, to discourage, to crush out of your life this sweet, sensitive plant, which would flower in your nature and give added glory to your life, for the sake of a few dollars, a little questionable fame?

Are the gift of life and the possibilities of man so cheap that we can afford to spend our existence in elbowing our way through life, crowding and jostling one another, trampling upon the weak in our mad greed and selfish ambition to rob them simply because we are stronger? Is might the right to which the higher civilization looks forward? If I plead for self-culture, self-improvement, for the development of the finest and the sweetest qualities of human nature, I must protest against the pace that kills them, the strenuous life that crushes them out, the mad haste, that tramples them under foot. It is incredible that men and women will pay such a price for things not worth while, that they will discard the imperishable in their rush for that which will fade and die.

Watch the typical business man in the early morning as he crosses the park, or common, or public garden, all radiant with beauty, which bids for his attention on every hand, while he walks rapidly along unconscious of it all. Masses of loveliness smile from flower beds, or blossom, or shrub, or tree, without attracting even a passing glance. He passes through the country when bird and brook and wild flower are vying with one another to arouse him from his absorption in business problems with the same careless indifference. People are so taken up with putting money into their purses that they have no time to put beauty into their lives. They are so absorbed in making a living that they have no time to make a life. Man cannot live by bread alone; his higher life demands an impalpable food.

"Few of us," says Sir John Lubbock, "realize the wonderful privilege of living; the blessing we inherit, the glories and beauties of the Universe, which is our own if we choose to have it so; the extent to which we can make ourselves what we wish to be; or the power we possess of securing peace, of triumphing over pain and sorrow."

We go through life with our eyes steadily fixed on a distant goal, straining every nerve to reach it. We pass on our way opportunities innumerable of helping others over rough places, of brightening and beautifying the commonplace life of every day. But we see them not. Heedless of all that does not help us on the line of our particular ambition we finally arrive at our destination to find — what? We have gained what we sought at the cost of all that sweetens and beautifies, ennobles and enriches life.

Fortunate indeed is the child who is trained to see beauty in everything and everywhere. An eye so trained is a perpetual magnifying glass revealing beauties invisible to the uncultivated eye. This self-culture, if properly conducted, will open up a thousand avenues of enjoyment beyond the reach of the ignorant. Let the youth be taught to look for beauty in all he sees, to embody beauty in all he does, and the imagination will then be both active and healthy. Life will be neither a drudgery nor a dream, but will become full of God's life and love.

SIR JOHN LUBBOCK.

IX.

LEARN TO EXPECT A GREAT DEAL OF LIFE.

AN infinite benefit comes from forming the habit of expecting the best of life for one's self. Do not go about with an expression of discontent on your face, giving everybody the impression that the good things of this world were intended for some one else. Practise the art of stretching your mind over great expectations. In this way you will broaden your position. If you learn the art of expecting great things for and from yourself, you are more likely to prepare yourself for great things. A sort of discontent has led to all the great things which have happened from the time of the earliest Hottentots to that of the Lincolns and the Gladstones.

No one can accomplish anything great in this world who is contented with little, who is confident that he was made for little things, or is satisfied with what happens to come in his way.

A man who expects great things of himself is constantly trying to open a little wider the doors of his narrow life, to extend his limited knowledge, to reach a little higher, to get a little farther on than those around him. He has enough of the divine disposition within him to spur him on to nobler endeavors. He looks to get the best of the things offered to him.

A false idea of what constitutes genius and real success

is one of the greatest stumbling-blocks in the way of youth's progress. It would be as reasonable for a mustard seed to refuse to grow because it never can become a pine, or for the grape-vine to refuse to extend its tendrils because it cannot become an oak, as for a boy to lose precious years hesitating and dallying because uncertain as to his possessing genius. The duty of the acorn is to become an oak, not a pine, not a rose. There is infinitely less of what is called real genius in the world than is generally supposed; that is, that genius which Joshua Reynolds declared to be "a power of producing excellences which are outside of the rules of art, a power which no prospect can touch and no industry acquire." Somehow, the average youth seems to think that there is breathed into some men a divine fire, a surpassing gift to do things without effort, thus violating all the laws of persistent industry; power to transmute common things into gold, a power akin to that of the Creator. The sooner one banishes from his mind all such nonsense the better.

Very few really successful men can give a satisfactory explanation as to why they pursued the course they are on. They seem to have been kept going by means of an unseen power. They simply acted in accordance with the best light they had.

No man can see the goal at the beginning. Even when he crosses the line in the race he can see only a few steps ahead. He is not guided by a star in the distance which beckons him on, but rather by a lantern which he carries in his hand, and which illumines but a short way in advance, just enough to enable him to take the next step with certainty and without fear. Beyond that all is shrouded in mist. But, as he travels on, the lantern never fails him.

When we are sure that we are on the right road there is no need to plan our journey too far ahead; no need to burden ourselves with doubts and fears as to the obstacles that may bar our progress. We cannot take more than one step at a time.

There is a perpetual inspiration in the effort to live one's best every day. To consider the whole of life at once is too much to grasp; but the effort to live one's best every day, to determine that for the day before us, at least, our ideal shall not be low-lying, but shall aspire, — this is practical right living, practical character-building.

Nothing else so strengthens the mind, enlarges the manhood, and widens the thought, as the constant effort to measure up to a high ideal, to struggle after that which is above and beyond us.

No matter what your work may be, or what you may do, put your ideal into it; be sure there is an upward tendency in it, an inspiring quality, a certain indefinable something which allies it to the divine.

Everybody loves an aspiring mind; a mind that looks up, never down, — out, never in, — no matter what difficulties confront it.

How quickly we can distinguish the aspiring from the grovelling mind! There is a certain indescribable charm about the person who has formed a habit of looking up; there is a superior quality in everything he does, no matter whether he be a congressman or a blacksmith.

"Did you ever hear of a man who had striven all his life faithfully and singly toward an object," asked Thoreau, "and in no measure obtained it? If a man constantly aspires is he not elevated? Did ever a man try heroism, magnanimity, truth, sincerity and find that there was no advantage in them, — that it was a vain endeavor?"

Aspiration finally becomes inspiration, and ennobles the whole life.

The most of us build Chinese walls around ourselves by our vicious thinking, our low ideals, unnatural living, separating ourselves from all that is best and sweetest in life. The stones in these walls are criticism, fault-finding, seeing the worst instead of the best in the world about us; they are made of worry, anxiety, trouble. We build these walls about us so high that they shut out the sunlight and we live in perfect darkness. No man can see over the wall which he erects over himself.

The character must feel the ideal; it is the aim which modifies the character and shapes the life. It influences motives, colors actions, determines destiny. The whole life points toward the ideal. If that is low, the life points downward, if high, it aspires. If they look towards the light, the faculties will look up; if towards the darkness, they will face night.

The leading aim will change the face to suit it, it will look out of the manner, it will speak from the bearing. What we long for and strive to attain, everybody who knows us can read; for we radiate our dominant aim. What we long to express in our life we are constantly expressing in our character. We radiate our purpose from every pore. Our ideal looks out of every voluntary act as much as our individuality inheres in every sentence of our handwriting and in our conversation. The ideal is constantly trying to become real, to out-picture itself upon the body in every act.

The real object of education and culture is to eliminate the brute nature and develop the real man. To attain this object everything depends upon choosing a high ideal at the very outset of life.

A grand character can never be developed under the shadow of a low, sordid aim. To look constantly to a high ideal is the only safe course for him who would become cultured and win real success. Manhood is a plant which thrives only in the sunshine of the soul. Its blossoms are chilled in a narrow, sordid, selfish atmosphere. The fruits of selfishness will surely kill the blossoms of perfection.

How little does a youth who starts out to make a fortune realize that the grasping passion to get and to hold will grow until it becomes a giant that will ultimately crush out all his finer sensibilities and nobler instincts! The man who is always scheming and planning to get the better of somebody else will unconsciously blight and wither up the qualities which, if nurtured, would bring into fruitage the principles of the Golden Rule.

The mind that is being constantly trained in shrewdness, sharpness, sagacity, cunning; that is ever on the alert to take advantage of a competitor's weakness; that is trained to see real value only in money and that which money can procure; to put the dollar mark on everything, to take advantage of others' weaknesses and misfortunes; in short, the training which teaches a youth to use those who have fallen in the race as stepping-stones to his own elevation is a process of education which develops only the brute qualities and dwarfs or wholly destroys soul-growth.

The supreme object of education and culture is to develop man along the line of his noblest nature, so that he will be not only keen, sagacious, and shrewd, but broad-minded, evenly and sympathetically balanced, tolerant, sweet, and charitable.

The properly educated youth will naturally express in his life the principles of the Golden Rule; he will recognize that others do not exist merely for his benefit; he will see that the highest good for each lies in mutual reciprocity. An education which does not achieve these results, which does not bring sweetness and light, harmony and power into the life, is no education at all.

It is one thing to succeed in business according to the ordinary acceptation; it is another and a totally different thing to succeed in life. Many a man has failed in business and yet lived a truly successful life, because he has lived up to his highest ideal. The man who does the very best he can under all circumstances, who makes the most of his ability and opportunities, who helps his fellow-man whenever it is in his power to do so, who gives the best of himself to every occasion, who is loyal and true in his friendships, kindly, charitable, and magnanimous toward all, is a successful man, though he may not leave enough money to pay his funeral expenses.

A noble character cannot be developed under the shadow of a low, sordid aim. The ideal must be high; the purpose strong, worthy, and true; or the life will be a failure. The man who is constantly scheming and planning to get the better of his neighbor, to drive a bargain in which the advantage will be all on his side, can never attain the dignity and grandeur of true manhood.

How many men who think they are succeeding by amassing fortunes are really failing to secure the very things for which they strive! While they are struggling to get that which they think will purchase nearly everything desirable, the true riches, without which all the money in the universe is but a mockery, elude their grasp.

Man is not a brute. To draw in and blow out the breath, or to eat and drink, is not living. A man cannot live by bread alone. The æsthetic faculties, the aspiring instincts, in a well-developed man, are ever more imperious in their demands for the true and the beautiful, for the higher and the nobler, than is the body for material food. It is as natural for the soul to aspire as it is for a blade of grass or a tree to grow upward.

> "What is man,
> If the chief good and market of his time
> Be but to sleep and feed? — a beast, no more:
> Sure He that made us with such large discourse,
> Looking before and after, gave us not
> That capability and god-like reason
> To rust in us unused."

When we see a boy or girl seizing every spare moment and every half holiday for self-improvement, when we see them gathering for self-enrichment the odds and ends of time which other boys and girls throw away, we are confident that they mean to gather riches which will not take wings. Wherever we see the disposition to make the most of one's self, to let no opportunity to add to one's self-culture pass, we feel sure that there we will find great returns, great wealth of character, of manhood or womanhood in the future.

Is there anything grander in this world than to see a young person who is bent upon self-enrichment, who is trying to make his life broader and sweeter and cleaner and truer, who is trying to be more of a man or more of a woman every day.

There is nothing impoverishing in the process of self-enrichment. If you are investing in helpfulness, in kindness, in unselfishness, in sympathy, in a longing to help everybody you come in contact with, to leave him a little higher up, a little further on, your life is growing richer and sweeter every day.

This is the kind of riches that endures, of wealth that lasts, — riches that fire cannot burn up, floods cannot wash away, which panics cannot affect. This is health that inheres in character. It is a part of manhood or womanhood. It is like gold, which no fire can consume or chemicals annihilate. The elements cannot touch it, calumny, detraction, abuse cannot tarnish it.

X.

MENTAL POWER.

THE development of mental power affords the best investment for a youth's capital,— his time and energy. It pays so to discipline one's mind as to discover what one can do best, and to form the mental habits which underlie success in life.

It does not pay to study Latin only a few weeks, "in order to get an insight into it;" to learn French in twelve lessons, if "the master will not plague the pupil with verbs and participles;" or to educate the family on the coöperative plan, "by a subdivision of Rome, the mother in picture galleries, the daughter at the monuments, and the father studying local color in the cafés."

We live in an age of haste. Some people seem to look at an egg, like the Chinese sage, "and expect to hear it crow." It is an era of "universities," "colleges," "professors,"— with "short courses" that lead no one knows whither. We behold around us educated men of an earlier generation who believed with Josh Billings that it is better not to know so many things than to know so much that is not so.

We rejoice in "university extension." It creates an atmosphere favorable for study and awakens the intellectual power of isolated pupils; yet the cramming of people's heads with facts leaves them uneducated, unless, in some other way, the power of original thinking is developed and the mind made ready to act upon the instant.

Education is mind-training for power. It is not only to sharpen one's tools, but also to make him who handles the tools more of a man.

"An education is no phonograph," says President Barrows, "to repeat mechanically what is poured into it, but a dynamo for the generation of power, for the illumination, movement, and gracious-handed comfort of mankind."

It is this kind of knowledge that enters into the mental bone and blood, so to speak, and it is the best paying investment. With our vast educational plant in America, expending four hundred million dollars a year, mind-training is power practically within every one's reach. Yet with nearly seventeen million pupils in our public schools very few advance beyond the highest grammar grade; and, so long as this is so, mind-training for power is the lot of the few, not of the many. Certainly it cannot be said, concerning those that do not study in the higher grades, that they are educated in the sense in which Plato understood it, — having that discipline "which gives to the body and to the soul all the beauty and all the perfection of which they are capable."

To make the most possible of one's self — discovering, developing his own powers, learning to use them to promote his own ends and the good of mankind — is the true purpose of man's education. It is the unfolding of nature, — of all that nature has given to him. It requires time and instrumentalities. To learn to think, to love the objects that ought to be loved, to direct the will to right ends, to observe, to reason, to exercise sound judgment, to control self, and to influence others, require time and teachers.

Nature does not make a specialist, a mere memory-gland or a money-gland, but her aim is a full-orbed man. If we develop the body exclusively, man deteriorates toward the brute. If we press all the vital energies of life into muscle-making we dwarf the soul and tear down manhood. It is an inexorable law of nature that what is exercised in one's daily vocation or as a special discipline becomes stronger. It was nature's intention that our faculties should be exercised in a healthy symmetrical manner. Any other course creates one-sidedness and discord. Cultivate the higher faculties of the brain alone, and expend all life's energies in expanding the power of the intellect, and what do we get? Not a full-orbed, well-rounded philosophy, but a cold, unsympathetic, one-sided mentality, devoid of all the finer graces, the warmer sympathies, the more delicate sentiments. Develop the moral nature alone, or even the spiritual, without the mental and the physical, and we have a fanatic, a zealot, an unbalanced enthusiast. The object of a watch is to keep as perfect time as possible. This time is not kept by the medium of any one tiny screw, or lever, or wheel, but is the resultant of the harmonious action of all, and depends upon the perfection of the minutest portion of the watch. So the object of all education and culture is the symmetrical development of all the legitimate faculties and functions.

This all-round development is best wrought by the systematic methods of the schools above the grammar grade, — the more grades the better. In saying this I do not undervalue the excellent work of the lower schools, or the discipline of regular work in the varied callings of subsequent life. I merely affirm what every one admits: that one's mental power is favored by larger schooling. Whether or not the methods of higher education are peculiarly adapted to every individual case, they are being constantly adapted to the average man; and they will pay him well for the investment of the time and labor necessary to utilize them.

"Perhaps the most valuable result of all education," said Huxley, "is the ability to make yourself do the thing you have to do when it ought to be done, whether you like it or not; it is the first lesson which ought to be learned, and, however early a man's training begins, it is probably the last lesson he learns thoroughly." Conformity to order, courage, and decision of character, and formation of the habits of industry, regularity, punctuality, thoroughness, persistency, patience, self-denial, intelligence in citizenship, and a wholesome self-respect, are characteristic of mind-training for power.

The practical working of a long course of schooling is thus shown by Professor Holden of the Lick Observatory in a quotation from a paper prepared by him on education at West Point:

"There is absolutely no favoritism in the treatment of the students by their instructors. Every academic performance is rated by a simple and effective marking-system, which is an essential part of the method of the school. This is an important point to notice. The very corner-stone of the most effective education is the marking-system. The marks of each cadet are publicly posted each week, so that he knows precisely what his own performance is worth. Absolute and complete justice is attained in this way more nearly than in any other organization which it has been my fortune to study. I have never heard it seriously questioned by any student, officer, or professor. The work of each cadet is therefore thoroughly tested every day, and no failure can possibly be hidden. The effect on the character of a student is immediate and admirable. He learns in the recitation-room, as everywhere else, not to shirk his duty; and he learns what few in civil life learn so early, that every shortcoming in the course of duty is sure to bring its corresponding penalty. A thoroughly unsatisfactory recitation not only receives a low mark, but is also treated as a dereliction of duty, and confinement to quarters on Saturday and Sunday afternoon is given as a punishment for such failures. High class-standing makes subsequent promotion in the army quick and certain. There is no moment when a cadet does not fully understand that his performance of duty now will influence his whole official career. This is fully recognized, and its perfect justice is admitted by all. The effect of diligence and faithfulness in the performance of allotted tasks is perfectly understood, and consequences follow actions with certainty. Every official delinquency has its appropriate number of demerit marks. Lateness at roll-call carries one demerit; absence, ten; slight untidiness in dress, one; inattention to duty or at drill, five, and so on.

"No cadet can have more than a certain small total number of demerits (some two hundred in a year) and remain in the academy. If he has more than the allowed total, he is dismissed. If he has fewer, his rank in his class is proportionately lowered, and his over privileges are curtailed, precisely as if he had failed in his studies. For an army officer good official conduct is at least as necessary as a knowledge of chemistry. Every delinquency is reported in writing, and each one involves a written explanation. Failure to render such an explanation is itself a delinquency. If the cadet has no excuse he must say so officially. If he has a sufficient excuse no demerit attaches to the offence. Each cadet must therefore examine his official conscience (so to speak) regularly, and record the results. All ill feeling is avoided, as the whole record is in writing and there are no personal reprimands.

"Let us now see how rigid a system this is. There are fifteen opportunities daily for a cadet to be late at roll-call. He is at the academy for about twelve hundred days. There are about eighteen thousand occasions during his four years' course on each one of which the regulations emphasize the duty of punctuality. If he is late, the offence carries one demerit. One hundred demerits in six months (one hundred and eighty days) will cause his dismissal. But tardiness is by no means the only delinquency. One button of his uniform-coat unbuttoned at drill, inattention, shoes not blacked at parade roll-call, gun not clean at guard-mount, and a hundred other matters of the sort, are parts of official conduct. Each failure is noted and carries with it a fixed number of demerits. One hundred demerits in six months dismiss him. All this is known to every one from the first. There is no talking. Only simple laws are prescribed. Each one of them is just. Every allowance is made for inexperience. Every reasonable excuse is admitted. The final result is like the result of gravitation, inevitable, inexorable, just, immediate."

West Point training is, in the end, specialized, being military. Other schools of advanced grade test men differently, but the result of the broadest education is mental power. A youth is seized upon, his capacities are discovered, his desire for knowledge is stimulated, and he is taught how to acquire it; the development of his own ability to go forward is the end sought, and he is prepared to take advantage of the boundless possibilities of life. He is not well educated who is not made morally better, more trustworthy, sweeter in spirit, more conscientious and of greater force in right living. It is this that gives the sense of a certain solidity of disciplined powers and that serenity of spirit and self-poise which we look for in man, who was created in the moral and spiritual image of his Maker.

It is as much a part of true education to develop appreciation and love of all forms of beauty and goodness, wherever found, as it is to learn grammar and arithmetic. Toleration, charity, and broad sympathy and love for our fellow-men are necessary parts of a true education. The most highly cultured man is he who has the greatest number of the highest products of the best mental development in the most refined form. Such a man is the highest mental expression of humanity. We should choose the things which have a high culture-value and appeal to the whole nature, giving an organic tone to the mind.

The great object of education is to raise man to his highest power. His springs are on high. His moving power is drawn from the fountains of living water.

The only real success worthy of the name is that which comes from a consciousness of growing wider, deeper, higher in mental and moral power as the years go on. To feel the faculties expanding and unfolding, to feel the leaven of the truth permeating the whole

being, is the only life worth living. Such a life is
neither drudgery nor a dream. It is rather the exquisite result of high qualities finely disciplined.

Many an extraordinary man has been made out of a
very ordinary boy; but, in order to accomplish this, we
must begin with him while he is young. It is simply
astonishing what training will do for a rough, uncouth,
and even dull lad if he has good material in him and
comes under the tutelage of a skilful educator before
his habits have been confirmed. Even a few weeks' or
months' drill of the rawest and roughest recruits in the
late Civil War so straightened and dignified stooping
and uncouth soldiers, and made them so manly, erect,
and courteous in their bearing, that their own friends
scarcely knew them. If this change is so marked in
a youth who has grown to maturity, what a miracle is
possible in the lad who is taken early and put under a
course of drill and systematic training, both physical,
mental, and moral. How many a man who is now in the
penitentiary, in the poorhouse, among tramps, or living
out a miserable existence in the slums of our cities,
bent over, uncouth, rough, slovenly, has possibilities
slumbering within his rags which would have developed
him into a magnificent man, an ornament to the human
race instead of a foul blot and scar, had he only been
fortunate enough early in life to have come under
efficient and systematic training.

Only four out of a hundred go to high schools,
academies, seminaries and business schools, and only
one-fourth of these go to college. Yet the colleges are
gaining in patronage. William T. Harris, United
States Commissioner of Education, states that in each
million of people the number of those receiving an

education above that of the grammar schools is three times as great as it was twenty-five years ago.

The necessity for earning money at an early age, or a passion for business on the part of young people in thrifty families, keeps many from pursuing longer courses of study. We often hear a father say that it is not necessary for his son to go to college in order to make money; as if mere wealth could be compared with an elevated, expanded, and ever-growing mind; as if money, with a narrow horizon, with a sordid and rutty life, can for a moment compare with the satisfaction which comes from being put into touch with all the world by a mind which has been electrified by a love for knowledge, and which has learned how to acquire it. Is it not the tendency of this age to put the interrogation point of commercial value upon everything? " Will the thing pay?" " What is there in it?" These are the questions too often asked. But what a mean, sordid view of life it is to look upon it as a mere mint for coining money, as if there were nothing higher or nobler for the grandest of God's creation than the piling up of wealth, the accumulating of houses and estates! Are the heart's yearnings, the soul's longings, to be satisfied with the piling up of material possessions?

There is something hardening, demoralizing, in the modern money-making career which tends to destroy all the finer instincts for the good, the beautiful, and the true, which dries up all sympathy for the misfortunes of others, dwarfs the growth of one's higher self, and crushes out the nobler impulses. One of the strangest and most unaccountable things in human experience is the fact that men will struggle and strive, day and night, for years and years, trying to make the most possible out of the farm, the shop, the trade, or the profession, — in other words, to develop their vocation to its utmost, to raise it to its highest point, — and yet utterly neglect the culture of their own higher powers.

The highest character, the noblest manhood, can never be developed under a low, sordid aim; and if a course in a college or a university could do nothing more than elevate the ideals and give a broader and truer outlook upon life, it would be well worth the time spent.

Every youth owes it to himself and to the world to make the most possible out of the stuff that is in him, to develop himself, not partially, not narrowly, nor in a one-sided way, but symmetrically, — in a large way. It is as much his duty to make the largest possible man of himself as it is the function of an acorn to become a grand oak, — not a little sapling, but a mighty tree which stands alone, buffets the storms and tempests, and furnishes shelter for man and beast and timber for the shipbuilders.

"We should so live and labor in our time," said Beecher, "that what came to us as seed may go to the next generation as blossom, and that what came to us as blossom may go to them as fruit."

HENRY WARD BEECHER.

XI.

IF YOU CAN TALK WELL.

IF you can express yourself clearly, in clean-cut, terse language, if you have the persuasive tone which fascinates and holds, you will have a powerful weapon. If it is attended by a fine manner, a gracious personality, you will have a passport everywhere; you will not need an introduction to the great, they will all welcome you. It seems strange that young people neglect the very art of arts, the power of conversation. Who can estimate it? The charm of a fine diction, the advantage of the power to talk well! Is n't it strange that our schools and colleges teach almost everything except the ability to use one's own language with power, with facility, with conviction? What accomplishments can for a moment compare with the ability to converse well, with all the charm of a powerful and fascinating speaker?

Students learn Latin and Greek and higher mathematics and theories which they may never or seldom use, but that which is brought into constant exercise almost every minute of their lives they never learn as a fine art. The average person's conversation is but an accident. They have never made it a study. They have picked up their vocabulary on the street, in the car, in the store, everywhere. They have never made a scientific study of words, their roots, origin, the meanings, their synonyms.

What comparison is there between an accomplishment which we use occasionally an that which we use all the time and everywhere, as we do conversational power? People will spend years and years working themselves almost to death to master some phase of art or of science, or literature, and yet so utterly neglect their power of conversation that they are very stupid and dull in society. Is n't it humiliating to be conscious of being a giant in your vocation and a pigmy or a dummy in the parlor, a mere nobody in society, so that you do not dare to open your mouth because you do not feel that you are master of your conversation? Is n't it humiliating to be in company and be obliged to sit in silence because a man or woman with one-tenth of your ability monopolizes the conversation, simply because he or she has cultivated the art which you have neglected?

Is n't it humiliating to sit dumb at a banquet to which you have been invited because of your reputation in some line of work? If called upon to speak you cannot express yourself as clearly and convincingly as a fifteen-year old boy ought to do. What matters it if you have discovered a new star, written a powerful book, invented a telephone, if you cannot say your soul is your own? It's a remarkable fact that men who have achieved great things in some special line do not dare to get up in an ordinary gathering to put a motion. They cannot preside at a public meeting for they have not the slightest idea of parliamentary rules. They would be frightened to hear their own voice in public; their limbs would tremble, and they would be all at sea, the mind confused like a child in its first attempt at declamation.

Isn't it humiliating, being conscious of knowing a great deal and not being able to express it? How clumsy the average man or woman is in conversation. They get snarled up in their sentences, twisted in their logic, and utterly confused when trying to put their thoughts clearly, to say nothing about elegant language.

Men may be a power in the office, but be mere children in social life. They have never learned to think on their feet; they could never hold the attention of an audience a minute; they are so dry, mechanical and uninteresting that nobody will listen to them. The merest tyro of a young boy or girl, gifted in talk, could take the attention of the company right away from them.

It does not matter what vocation you choose, if you cannot talk well, if you have not the gift of self-expression, if you cannot use language suited to the occasion, you will always be placed at a disadvantage.

Many people pass for a great deal more than they are because of their elegance of expression, their fine diction, — they can express themselves. They may have but one talent, but they make the most of it, they knew how to call out their mental reserves, and to use them to advantage.

How many people owe their advancement, their position, largely to their ability to talk well. Making a good appearance, a favorable first impression, is everything, and no one can do this so well as a good, charming talker. How many men in public life owe their success and popularity largely to their fine conversational powers. Many a man has lifted himself to Congress or into a governorship, or other high office, by his ability to talk well. Many a man has talked himself into a good position and a fine salary. Their ability alone would never have carried them there.

It is a great treat to converse with a man or woman who is master of this art. Their voices are like music in our ears, they have the power to charm, to soothe us, to satisfy, like a beautiful face or form. Many peoples' vocabularies are composed of all sorts of incongruities. They have never been taught the magic of choosing just the right shade of words — just the right meaning. A one-talent man who has learned to use his tongue, — has learned to fascinate, to interest, to succeed in holding attention. We know men and women who have developed this art to such an extent that wherever they go they command instant recognition. They are listened to in whatever company they appear; everybody else keeps silent, they cannot help listening.

Conversation is an art in which one may employ every bit of his skill and experience. You can tell how widely a man has travelled, whether he is a close or a slipshod observer; you can tell whether he is a systematic or a slovenly man. You can see what books he has read, and how he has read them, in his conversation. You can select his companions, you know his associates; you can tell where he has been, and what he has done. You can trace the trend of his thought, his habits of life, in what he says and how he says it. It is an art which embraces all others. No matter what your life has been, how much you know, where you have been, what you have done, you can find it all out in your conversation. It adheres to your word, it sticks to your compressed thought, they are all telltales of your life. Your conversation is a perfect panorama of your experiences. We know whether you are ignorant or learned, whether a giant or a pigmy, whether fine or coarse, sympathetic or selfish by what you say.

Conversational power every young person, who expects to accomplish anything in the world, should acquire; he should be able to command himself perfectly, to converse with ease and elegance in company. To be able to interest people is a great achievement in itself. It is worth everything to the youth who would achieve anything of note. This reputation will help him all through his life. How often when a man is wanted for an important position some one will say, "Let's send Mr. Smith, or appoint him for this or that place. He will represent us with dignity because he knows what to say, he knows how to make a good impression, a good appearance."

Conversation is a great educator. A good conversationalist brings into play a great many qualities. He must exercise his tact. His judgment comes into play. Good sense can never be absent. The good conversationalist must be large-hearted, generous; if mean, if narrow, if prejudiced, all his bad qualities, as well as his good ones, come out in conversation. He must have a warm sympathy for his listeners. He must be interested in them, he must tactfully avoid their sore spots, or exposing their weaknesses. His power of analysis is in constant use. His creative ability must be exercised also. A good talker cannot be an imitator, a mere echo.

We advise young people to resolve at the very outset that, whatever else they do, they will cultivate the art of conversation at every opportunity. The ability to talk well is a tremendous power to a man who can command attention in any company.

It is pitiable to see how some able men and women

stammer and wrestle with the English language, botching their sentences, mixing the parts of speech, dropping their adjectives and verbs as though they had never attempted to put a sentence together before.

It ought to be the ambition and pride of every young man and woman to handle language with facility and power, to express themselves vigorously, concisely, forcefully. The cultivation of a fine diction is an enviable acquirement.

Whatever other ambition you may have, resolve that you will become a specialist in conversational ability. You cannot practise law, medicine or any other profession, or attend to business, but you have a chance every day to bring into use your powers of speech, always and everywhere, and it is a shame with so many opportunities that you cannot become an adept. One of the best possible investments you can make is to spend time in studying the dictionary, tracing words, their roots, their origins, studying the thesaurus for synonyms and equivalent expressions, in order to give variety and breadth to your conversation, trying to broaden your vocabulary in every possible way, looking up every word which you come across that you do not know. This is an education in itself; it will mean very much to you. You cannot be a good converser with a narrow vocabulary or a limited experience. It takes breadth and largeness of view to be a conversationalist. The narrow, fault-finding, backbiting, criticising person, the sour pessimist, can never charm. The noble qualities must preside or the conversation will be lean and pinched.

XII.

BREVITY AND DIRECTNESS.

I saw one excellency was within my reach,— it was brevity, and I determined to obtain it. — JAY.

WHEN I went into a New York business house, recently, this confronted me, and drove its lesson forcibly home. A little later, in Chicago, I ran across a similar warning not to waste the time of business people: —

BE BRIEF !
WE HAVE OUR LIVING TO MAKE, AND IT TAKES
CONSIDERABLE OF OUR TIME TO DO IT.

Such posted notices show two things, — the immense value in modern life of dispatch and quick performance of business, and the presence in business of a lot of persons whose sole visible mission seems to be to prevent this being done. The day of the bore and the long-winded discourser is past, and these mottoes furnish a polite way of telling these time-wasters what could not be told in words without offence. Modern methods have no place, no tolerance for them.

If there is anything that exasperates a business man it is to try to do business with men who never get anywhere, who never come to the point, who "beat about the bush" with long introductions and meaningless verbiage. Like a dog which turns around a half dozen times and then lies down where he was in the first place, they tire one out with useless explanations, introductions, and apologies, and talk about all sorts of things but the business of the moment.

There are some men you never can bring to the point. They will wander all around it, over it and under it, always evading and avoiding, but never quite touching the marrow. Their minds work by indirection; their mental processes are not exact. They are like children in the play called " Poison," — they try to avoid touching the designated object. It seems unaccountable that people will take so much trouble apparently to avoid coming to the point.

The business caller who takes his ease, lounges down in a chair, and talks familiarly of anything that comes into his systemless head, is nowadays sure to kill the success of the business he is trying, in his weak and inefficient way, to put through. Modern business is touch-and-go, take it or leave it, if you don't want it somebody else does. Every moment of a business interview should be applied to the object in hand, the matter under consideration. Some people, however, do not seem to have the ability to come right squarely up to the point at issue. Judges and lawyers say that it is practically impossible to get from some witnesses the information wanted on a certain point. Though the attorney may resort to all sorts of ingenious methods to get a direct answer, the witnesses will not commit themselves. They talk all around the point, go almost up to it on every side, but stop short of it or avoid it.

I know a business man who is so indirect and long-drawn-out in his conversation that I almost always get out of patience while doing business with him and wondering if he is ever going to finish, and can hardly resist constant reference to my watch. When he calls me by telephone, I feel like leaning back in my chair and elevating my feet, because I know I must sacrifice at least a quarter of an hour of valuable time right in the midst of business hours. Such people are nuisances. More or less of this long-drawn-out quality, lack of directness and pointedness, is to be expected in professional men and in women, but it is a fatal quality for an ambitious young business man. It is a success-killer. Men who get through a large amount of work, men of great executive ability, are quick, concise, accurate, pointed.

I have another business friend, very successful, who calls me by telephone, and, without any preliminaries, proceeds right to the subject, states his proposition, and, almost before I can think what he has said, says "Goodby," and is gone. It is a perfect luxury to do business with such a man. He never bores you, never tires you. I never see this friend without feeling great admiration for his mental alertness, prompt decision, and efficiency. This executive quality is not difficult to cultivate if one begins early and knows his defects. One should train himself constantly to concentrate his thoughts, to crystallize his business into concise, clean-cut sentences.

In no other way will a man betray lack of the quality of dispatch so much as in his correspondence. It can often be detected in the first sentence of an unbusinesslike letter. I have corresponded with people on important matters for weeks, writing letter after letter asking the same question, urging that it be answered directly, and yet, every time it was evaded, apparently not intentionally, but just as surely and aggravatingly.

Business letters should be models of condensation, crystallized into a few sentences. Compactness, comprehensiveness and pointedness are characteristics of the letters of a successful man of affairs, who will say more in a dozen lines than another can write on two pages. A single letter from a man we have not seen betrays the whole structure of his mind.

It is said that Agassiz, from a tiny bone, from a foot, perhaps, could reproduce an entire prehistoric animal, giving its habits, telling what kind of food it subsisted upon, where it lived, etc., even if it was extinct before man came upon the earth. Just so an observant person can, from a letter, a brief conversation, a telegraphic or telephonic message, describe the structure of the individual's mind, whether narrow or broad, logical or illogical, orderly or disorderly, can tell you of his mental habits, and whether he is clean-cut or a slipshod and slovenly man.

It is a good drill, in business correspondence, to imagine that you are writing a cablegram where every word costs twenty-five cents, and to try to express the greatest amount of the thought in the fewest words. After you have written a letter or an essay as concisely as you think possible, go over it again and erase every superfluous word, recasting the sentences. By studying brevity of expression, one will soon overcome the slipshod habit of spreading over a page many sentences containing only a straggling, illogical thought. Such practice will also greatly improve the quality of one's thinking. Brevity should also be applied to conversation, effort being made to see how few words can be made to express the greatest idea. Begin very near where you mean to leave off.

Many a boy has failed to obtain a good situation by answering an advertisement with a sprawling, slipshod letter; and many a man owes his success to a concise application for a position. I have seen business men, in looking over a large number of applications for a situation, set aside a single letter because of its neatness, compactness, and brevity of statement. The practised eye of the employer saw in that letter that its author was a young man of executive promise although he had never seen him, while a long-drawn-out letter, covering pages of self-laudation, did not attract him. He knew that the boy would correspond with his letter, and the letter of a few lines, which said a great deal, made a strong and favorable impression.

When boys and young men ask my opinion about their ability to succeed in business, I try to find out whether they have this power of directness, of coming to the point clearly, squarely, and forcibly without indirection, without parleying, without useless words. If they lack this quality, apparently there is little chance of their succeeding in a large way, for this is characteristic of men of affairs who achieve great things. The indirect man is always working to disadvantage. He labors hard, but never gets anywhere. It is the direct man who strikes sledge-hammer blows, the man who can penetrate the very marrow of a subject at every stroke and get the meat out of a proposition who does things.

The same is true of authors. The ever-living authors have expressed their thoughts in transparent language. They have stripped the expression of their ideas of verbiage, of all superfluity. They have chosen words which exactly fit the thought. They have left no traces of anything perishable which time can corrode or affect, and so they live always. What power will time ever have to erase a single sentence from Lincoln's immortal speech at Gettysburg, Longfellow's "Psalm of Life," or Shakespeare's divine creations? How many centuries and ages, think you, would obliterate Christ's story of the lilies of the field, or the Sermon on the Mount, or Gray's "Elegy"?

The greatest writers have spent hours hunting for a word which would give the exact delicacy of expression desired, or an entire day rewriting, rearranging and polishing a single line in a poem. In a letter, which one of these immortals wrote to a friend, he said, in speaking of his work: — "I am still at it at the rate of a line a day." *Nulla dies sine linea.*

Some imperishable poems and immortal bits of prose have been elaborated during years of thought and patient endeavor for fitting expression which would stand the test of time. Men who have written for immortality have put weeks, months, years, perhaps, into a poem or a chapter. There are writers who have gained fame with a few brief sentences, a stanza or verse, while others who have written scores of volumes are forgotten before they die. Limpidity of thought and directness of language have frequently been the determining factors of such fame or oblivion.

Young writers attribute Kipling's fame to unusual genius. No doubt he has a great deal of natural ability, yet many of these young writers would not deign to rewrite a story from eight to ten times, as Kipling does, in order to express his thought in the most forceful, telling, and most concise manner before giving it to the public. They would expect, with a tithe of his experience and carefulness, to write a story in a few hours and then feel hurt because it was returned with thanks. An editor can tell very quickly whether a manuscript bears the stamp of concentrated thought and persistent endeavor, for every sentence betrays the writer's mind. An editor's experienced eye detects a looseness of expression, a lack of balance and mastery in the use of language. He notes feverish haste, scorning patient endeavor to find proper words, and sees the lack of finish. Such defects influence his decision. He sees the traces of effort which true art always conceals, and every unnatural straining after effect, and lack of simplicity and conciseness in treatment. The trouble with most writers is that they are "addicted to language," — their thought is covered up with words, words, words. They should take the advice of Tryon Edwards, —" Have something to say, and stop when you're done."

XIII.

FROM AN EDITORIAL POINT OF VIEW.

YOUNG writers often regard editors as their worst enemies, and seem to think that they take delight in returning manuscripts, when, as a matter of fact, good composition and well-written manuscript are like nuggets of gold to them. They are always hunting for something distinctly good, something strong, original in plan, and with real merit, which will be helpful, and will attract attention. They return unavailable manuscripts with a feeling of disappointment at failure to find what is sought, mingled with disgust at the wretched quality of the offerings of unskilled, untrained, careless writers.

The art of expressing one's self on paper is one of the grandest, but one of the most difficult to acquire, and yet people who would not think of attempting to play on a piano in public until they had practised for weeks, or even months, will sit down, and in a few hours throw off an article, send it to a leading publication, and then be surprised when it is returned. To attain the power to express your heart's longings, your soul's aspirations, to enable you to voice your hopes and aspirations, to describe life as you see it, is the work of years of hard and persistent practice, just as musical excellence is.

The editors of most magazines return with thanks about ninety-nine articles and stories out of every hundred submitted. The young writer cannot understand why his article is returned, as it seems so complete to him, so well-balanced, and his fine thoughts are so beautifully expressed, but the experienced editor sees that the novice has been writing in a circle; he notes the narrowness of experience, the paucity of thought, the poverty of language, the limitations of vocabulary. He sees how little the writer has travelled or experienced, how ignorant he is of human nature, of the philosophy of life. Many of the articles sent to magazines would disgrace a high school pupil. They lack style and continuity of thought, and are without point or purpose. The great majority lack individuality.

Many of the manuscripts returned show evidence of ability, of earnestness, of real merit, but they are too often written in a loose-jointed, slipshod manner. Others are evidently produced without enthusiasm, knowledge, or confidence, simply to gain financial profit if possible. They show signs of haste and carelessness and are written without thoroughly considering or pre-adjusting the material. Editors are too busy to re-write articles, no matter how promising the material, and so must reject good matter if badly presented. Half-heartedness and lack of purpose characterize some of the articles. Some lack thought and are mere word-pictures. Many of them lack plan and arrangement. Such are a mere jumble of incidents and commonplace expressions. A great many young writers of ability fail from this lack of order in their thoughts and writings. They jumble everything together, helter-skelter, all in a pile. Many of them have good ideas, but, not knowing how to differentiate them, they are spoiled by the manner of expressing them. Such writers seem to have little idea of logical sequence. Their articles have no introduction, middle or end, and yet they expect their work to be accepted and read with interest and applause. A dry goods merchant might as well expect to sell goods by tumbling them helter-skelter all about his store, regardless of order or arrangement, with shoes and thread, silks and groceries all mixed, on the theory that a customer would find what he wished for.

Comparatively few writers have learned the art of condensation. They string their thoughts out till it is difficult to find the trace of an idea. You can drive a horse and cart through many of their sentences they are so loosely constructed. Such writers do not realize that even an inch of space in a large publication is worth many dollars, and that condensation, clearness, and terseness of expression are everything to a good editor.

The greatest writers economize most of the reader's attention. They do not leave anything for the reader to do that they can possibly do for him. They do not cover up their thought by useless verbiage, or by circumlocution. It lies transparent on the surface in clear, simple, limpid language. Good composition is easy reading; the thought is not obscured by big words or by involved sentences. Readers tire of most authors trying to find out what they are driving at. No man likes to work hard reading a book. One cannot afford to dig out thought from verbose language, intricate and interminable sentences — this is the work of the author, not of the reader. If the writer has not served his ideas in an attractive, fascinating style, if he does not hold the reader irresistibly to his thought, he has failed. Many young writers mistake language for ideas, quantity for quality. Many modern writers would fill a whole library trying to express the thoughts that Emerson crowded into a few volumes.

Dairymen tell us that in order to keep butter sweet indefinitely, every particle of foreign matter, every bit of buttermilk which could possibly become rancid must be worked out of it; so ideas and thoughts, to become immortal, must be stripped of every bit of superfluous expression. Language must be simple and transparent; ideas must be expressed directly in the fewest possible words if you wish your work to live.

If a young writer would only start out holding constantly in mind the determination to save the reader's time, to economize his attention by cutting out every useless word, reducing every sentence to the fewest possible words, condensing everywhere, he would not only get a most helpful lesson in composition, but also his articles and books would be read and praised. The young writer will find splendid practice in rewriting many times an article or chapter, even after he thinks it is well done, trying each time to express the thought more forcibly, in simpler language, in less space, and still without loss of ideas. He will be much helped in this process if he will imagine that he must send his article by cable and pay a quarter of a dollar for every word. He will be surprised to see how many words he can spare, how many repetitions he has made. He will be surprised and pleased to see how effectively he can express an idea in more concise sentences by continual recasting.

No one can write with power who is not full of his subject, completely permeated with it. Readers can tell very quickly whether you are a specialist, whether you speak with authority born of long study and investigation, or whether you speak in echoes of another writer's thought. If your knowledge of the subject you treat is limited you cannot conceal the fact, your ignorance will show through as bread shows through butter too thinly spread. Do not think that you can read a little about the matter, and just touch the surface of your subject here and there, and thus captivate your readers. You will do nothing of the kind; every sentence that you write will indicate the superficiality of your knowledge, the meagreness of your study, and the poverty of your thought.

Enthusiasm, a requisite for interesting, forceful composition, is impossible to a superficial student. To be carried away with a subject, to have a soul all aglow with interest and enthusiasm, you must know it through and through, and you must come to its expression in the spirit of a lover and not that of a slave. Write because you love to write, and not because you have to, because you have something to say and not because you wish to say something. You must feel a mission to write before you can say anything worth reading. You cannot make your reader feel what you do not first feel yourself. If you are not stirred to the very depth of your being by your subject, if your feeling does not tingle on the very tip of your pen, if it does not flow in your ink, you cannot expect your reader to be moved. He will be cold as an icicle if you are indifferent. You cannot rivet his attention upon a page which you wrote without intense feeling.

What a difference there is in the composition of authors! I have just been reading a bit of writing, every word of which seemed like a live wire, full of electricity, running over with energy. Every line sent a thrill through me as I read it. I went over it again and again, and each time I felt the shock. Every perusal was a fresh tonic, rousing the mental faculties, stirring the soul to its centre. I could feel every experience of the writer. Every thrill of joy, every blow of sorrow, everything which had entered into his life seemed to quiver in his words. The whole page seemed to be throbbing with human interest, warm with sympathy, pulsating with life. I could almost write the writer's life from his pages, for they seemed to be a part of him, a panorama of his experiences. Every sentence seemed a cross-section of some part of the author's life. I could see the man stand out on his pages almost as clearly as if he really stood before me.

XIV.

THAT FEELING OF SMALLNESS.

One of the most demoralizing things we know of is the habit of berating one's self. Some people are always doing this. They seem to delight in telling how little they amount to, and how insignificant they are in comparison with others.

The churches are largely responsible for this self-depreciation. How often we hear in prayer-meetings this constant berating of one's self People call themselves miserable sinners, poor worms of the dust instead of the kings, the queens, the men, the women God made. Clergymen in pulpits and people in prayer-meetings often tell the Lord how insignificant they are. Instead of boldly claiming their birthright of nobility, of royal manhood and womanhood, they whine and apologize and crawl. Man was made erect that he might stand up, look up, look the world in the face without wincing. This acting the Uriah Heep before the Creator is despicable and demoralizing.

If the Bible teaches anything it bids man to look up, to claim his birthright. What would a father think of his son if he should come to him with a request in a humiliating spirit of self-depreciation? The father wants him to come with all his dignity and manhood intact.

This habit of self-depreciation is demoralizing to one's character. It destroys self-confidence, kills independence and makes a man vertebrateless.

Self-depreciation destroys that dignity, that beauty of poise and balance which characterize the true gentleman. Some people have a regular genius for self-effacement. They skulk round always trying to keep in the back seats or out of sight as much as possible wherever they go, but there is something in human nature which despises sneaking. The world loves the man who has the courage to stand erect, to think his own thoughts, to live his own life, and to call himself every inch a man.

" No man," says Emerson, " can be cheated out of an honorable career in life unless he cheats himself." You will not cheat yourself unless you cease to believe in yourself; a noble estimate of life and of one's self is a powerful projector of character. Do not start out in life with a contemptible estimate of yourself.

One reason you have failed to assert yourself is perhaps because you have been disgusted with nervy people who substituted cheek for ability, and you determined to assume a non-pretentious, humble air; but self-effacement never yet made a man, and never will. There is much difference between disagreeable, bragging conceit based upon cheap vanity or false pride, and real confidence based upon a knowledge of ability and honest conviction that we are capable of doing the thing we undertake.

Self-respect, a good opinion of your own personality, is the best insurance not only against vile, vicious tendencies, but also against making a wrong choice and against final failure. A man who thinks highly of himself will not stoop to underhanded methods, to low, vile scheming. No matter what your calling, preserve your self-respect at all hazards; let your money go, let your property go, part with everything material, but hold to your self-respect.

XV.

YOUR MOST VALUABLE POSSESSION.

NOTHING else is worth so much to you as your unqualified endorsement of yourself. The approval of the "still, small voice" within you, which says to every noble act, "That is right," and to every ignoble one, "That is wrong," is worth more to you than all the kingdoms of the earth. It matters little what others may think about you or what the world may say; it makes no difference whether the press or the public praises or blames; it is by your own honest judgment of yourself that you must stand or fall.

Many a man who is looked upon as successful, lauded in the daily papers, sought after by society, and looked up to by his wealthy neighbors, knows perfectly well that he is a fraud. His heart never beats but it disapproves of his deception. Every time he is reminded of his success,—in dollars and cents,—his conscience pricks him. Every time he goes through his factory or mines, the wan faces, emaciated forms, starved and cramped lives whose blood is on every dollar of the huge fortune which their ill-requited toil has enabled him to amass, sternly accuse him. They tell him in thunder tones, that, instead of being the great success which the world thinks him, he is a gigantic failure, and that his wealth has been acquired literally at the cost of human lives. He realizes that their accusations are just. He has murdered the opportunities, crushed the ambitions, and prevented the adequate education of hundreds of young toilers who are little better than his chattel slaves. Forced into the battle of life to help eke out the miserable pittance earned by their fathers or mothers, or both parents, they have never known childhood or freedom or happiness.

Can such an employer, no matter how seared his conscience, be happy when he meets the glances of those disappointed eyes, and when he contrasts the miserable surroundings of those unfortunate children who labor in order that his own little ones may be surrounded with luxury? Can he enjoy his wealth when he rides in his luxurious carriage, accompanied by a coachman and a footman, past the miserable homes of those poor people? Will not the pleading eyes of those unfortunate children, whose spiritual lives he has crushed, and who have never had even the ghost of a chance to develop their dormant possibilities, haunt his dreams? Will not those accusing faces rise up before him at the banquet table, in the midst of the applause of the multitude, and condemn him?

There is no alchemy by which the man who has not earned his own approval can extract real happiness and true satisfaction from either his money or his position.

Be sure, then, that you have your own approval first and last. If you resolve that you will never forfeit confidence in yourself, and that you will never take chances of your own disapproval, whatever you have or do not have, you will have a bulwark which will be your stay whether in prosperity or in adversity.

At the least murmur of disapproval of the "still,

small voice" halt and ask yourself what you are about to do and whither you are going. There is something wrong, — of that you may be sure. You must remedy it immediately. Don't parley with the cause of your disturbance; don't try to compromise with it. Such a course will prove as dangerous as that of a mariner who, in the midst of a storm, should insist upon holding the needle to a certain point by force because he wanted to sail in that direction. To try to influence the compass would be to wreck his ship upon the rocks or shoals in his path. There are human wrecks all along the ocean of life who have disregarded or tried to compromise with their compass, — conscience.

To keep your self-approval you must be honest. It is impossible to be dishonest and not stand condemned before the bar of conscience. No matter how slight the departure from truth or integrity, no matter how trifling the deception or untruthfulness (if any deception or untruthfulness can be considered slight), you have been tampering with the needle and, if you persist in such a course, you will not reach the harbor you seek.

You cannot sell shoddy for all wool, thirty-two inches for a yard, thirty quarts for a bushel, or domestic for imported goods; you cannot cheat your employer of time or service or by not giving the best that is in you without compromising with your conscience.

If you keep your self-approval, no matter what other things you may lose, you will still be rich. You may make a fortune or you may lose one; you may live in a beautiful home or in a cheap boarding house; you may wear rich garments or cheap ones; you may ride in a fine carriage or you may walk; you may keep your friends or you may lose them; you may have the good opinion of the world or its contempt, but, if you have never tampered with your conscience, if you believe in yourself, if you approve of your life, if you have been honest and earnest and true, and if you can look yourself square in the face without wincing, you will be happy and successful, even though the world should brand you as a failure.

How many people who are living in fine houses, riding in elegant carriages, and spending money like water trying to enjoy themselves, would give half, yea, some of them all, of their wealth in exchange for their bartered self-approval.

It is said that the basest criminal feels a sense of consciousness of justice, and says "Amen" in his heart, while he feels the words, "That is right, that is right," quivering on his lips, when the judge pronounces his doom. This voice is his own best self which never forsook him, and which, had he obeyed its warnings, would have brought him to victory as surely as the sun brings flowers and fruitage to the earth.

No matter how poor a man is as long as he is progressing, however slowly, his life is healthy and he has hope. But the moment a man ceases to progress, when he ceases to grow higher, wider, and deeper, when he has ceased to acquire power to get on, then his life becomes stagnant and mean.

In the evolution of the saint there is a perpetual striving, — a divine dissatisfaction.

The noblest character would soon degenerate if it should lose the love of excellence. This is the mainspring of all great character. This passion for excellence is the voice of God, bidding us up and on, lest we forget our Divine origin and degenerate to barbarism again. This principle is the guardian of the human race. It is God's voice in man; it is the still, small voice that whispers "right" or "wrong" to every act; it is the gem which the Creator dropped into the dust when he fashioned us in His own image.

Bury a pebble and it will obey the law of gravitation forever. Bury an acorn and it will obey a higher law and grow. In the acorn is a vital force superior to the attraction of the earth. All plants and animals are climbing or reaching upward. Nature has whispered into the ear of all existence: "Look up." Man, above all, should have a celestial gravitation. The ambition of every true man should be to be more, not to have more.

No man can be mentally, morally, and physically healthy until his ambition is satisfied. There must be contentment, satisfaction which comes from the consciousness of being in one's place where all of the faculties pull, — not a few of the weaker ones. The emergencies must be very exceptional, the environment extremely rare which will justify you in trying to get a living where you hear the highest and best in you constantly reminding you that you are sacrificing them. But there is a healthful tonic which comes from the healthful exercise of the strongest thing in you. There is a satisfaction, a sense of completeness, of wholeness, of fitness of things which can never come from living-getting by the weak faculties.

It is impossible to do an unmanly act, however secretly, although no one in the world may seé or know it, without a corresponding deterioration of the character. Is n't it a pitiable sight to see a healthy, strong, able, educated man trying to get a living by qualities which he should suppress, — by cunning, longheadedness, greed, planning and scheming to outwit others, to hypnotize them by lying advertisements, by false statements. It seems strange that people should not choose vocations which call out their highest and noblest qualities, which give the largest education and the broadest culture as well as a living, instead of choosing that which will warp their natures, stunt their manhood, starve all their nobler sentiments and blunt their finer qualities. When we learn that a vocation means man-making even more than living-making then we shall begin to live.

Whatever one may learn from books, whatever from his occupation, whatever from observation, it is probably an indisputable fact that he absorbs more of that which may most properly be called culture, wisdom, or unwisdom, morality or immorality, refinement or vulgarity, chastity or unchastity, from his habitual associates, than in any other way, or in all other ways put together.

"We take the color of the society we keep," says Geikie, "as the tree-frogs do that of the leaf on which they light, or as Alpine birds change with winter or summer. The east wind strips the spring's blossoms; the warm south wind opens them into clouds of pink. Ask Shame and Guilt and they will tell you they were made what they are by Example and Intercourse; and, on the other hand, Honor and Usefulness commonly hasten to own that they owe everything, humanly speaking, to some one they have copied."

There are, of course, exceptions to this as to every other rule, but they are exceedingly few. We are, for the most part, mirrors, and can reflect but what we have seen, — the ugly and the beautiful in life. We are but

PHILLIPS BROOKS.

whispering galleries which give back only the echoes of what we have heard.

It is a truth of which to be grateful, that the good is as easily and deeply absorbed as the bad. Millions of noble men and women date the beginning of their nobility from the time they first knew certain people. Everyone who came into even transient companionship with Phillips Brooks went away with something more of worth in his character. "I scarcely ever meet President Andrews," said a student at Brown University, "but I am better for being in his atmosphere."

An Oriental poem conveys, in a fascinating manner, this idea of mental and spiritual absorption:

> "A fragrant piece of earth salutes
> Each passenger, and perfume shoots,
> Unlike the common earth or sod,
> Around through all the air abroad.
> A pilgrim once did near it rest,
> And took it up and thus addressed:
> 'Art thou a lump of musk? or art
> A ball of spice, this smell t' impart
> To all who chance to travel by
> The spot where thou, like earth, dost lie?'
> Humbly the clod replied: 'I must
> Confess that I am only dust.
> But once a rose within me grew;
> Its rootlets shot, its flowerets blew;
> And all the rose's sweetness rolled
> Throughout the texture of my mold;
> And so it is that I impart
> Perfume to thee, whoe'er thou art.'"

XVI.

SUPERIORITY THE BEST TRADE-MARK.

MEN spend large sums of money and a great deal of thought, nowadays, in protecting the products of their brains and their hands by patents and copyrights, and even then their ideas are appropriated and imitated by others. There is one safe way, however, by which we can protect the work of our brains and muscles, and that is by superiority — doing things a little better than anybody else can do them.

Stradivarius did not need any patent on his violins, for nobody else was willing to take such pains to put the stamp of superiority upon his instruments. Plenty of other makers were content to make cheap violins, and they ridiculed Stradivarius for spending weeks and months on an instrument when they could turn one out in a few days. Stradivarius was determined to make his name worth something on a violin — to make it a trade-mark which would protect it forever — the stamp of his character, of honest endeavor — this was his patent, his trade-mark. He needed no other.

The name of Graham on a chronometer was protection enough, because nobody else at that time could make such a perfect timepiece. He learned his trade of Tampian, of London, probably the most exquisite mechanic in the world, whose name on a timepiece was proof positive of its excellence.

Joseph Jefferson has been all the protection the play, "Rip Van Winkle," has required for a quarter of a century, for he has stamped such superiority upon his part that no one else has ever approached it.

The name of Tiffany on a piece of silverware or jewelry has been all the protection it has needed for half a century.

The name of Huyler, who, as a boy, began by peddling molasses candy from a basket in the streets of New York, placed upon a package of confectionery, has been a protection almost equal to a patent for a great many years.

Such names, which are synonymous with honesty, are equal to any trade-mark or patent whenever and whereever they are found. Nobody thinks of going back of them or inquiring into the quality or reliability of goods so marked. These names stand for character, which is the consummate protector and best advertisement, and they are mentioned with respect. How often is the contrary noted, — a contemptuous reference to a man or a firm whose name is known to be synonymous with inferiority, and who tries to palm off just as paltry goods or talent or service as can force acceptance. We never have respect for a man who deals in imitations or who manufactures or sells shoddy as we have for one who deals in genuine articles. The human mind loves the actual, the real, the genuine, the things that ring true, and hates the false.

Note the difference between the character of the maker and seller of articles of merchandise that are noted for their superiority and that of the man who spends a lifetime in the barter of cheap make-believe goods, who constantly tries to make things appear what they are not, — to cover up base metal with a thin wash of gold, and to imitate diamonds with paste.

To spend a life buying and selling lies, or cheap shoddy shams, whether in jewelry, clothing, furniture, stocks, or bonds, is demoralizing to every element of nobility, — to excellence in any form.

There is a vast difference in the character of even the employees in a place like Tiffany's and in stores of the imitation-diamond and cheap-jewelry dealers. It does not matter that they do not make or sell imitations, the very fact that they deal with false things affects them. The quality of the sham is caught by the employees through familiarity with the inferior and through need of employing pretence in dealing with customers.

It is demoralizing to have any share in dishonest, shoddy work. There is enough of the good, the true, and the beautiful to do, so you need not ally yourself with their opposites. Ally yourself with a house that stands for something high and makes and sells substantial goods.

"Never put your name to a certificate or a piece of work unless you know it is worthy," said Senator George F. Hoar in an address to students; "throw up your job first. Let no employer's command move you to do that which you know is wrong. The city of Lowell was built on the Merrimac River. Dams and canals were constructed to conserve the water power. There was no competent engineer for such work in America at that time. A young Englishman named Francis came over and was employed. He looked over the work already done. He learned that, sixty years before, there had been a great flood in the valley. He went to the directors of the company. 'Gentlemen,' he said, 'you must rebuild Lowell and the works.'

"'We can't do that,' was the answer; 'we have spent large sums and must take a risk.'

"'Then, gentlemen,' said Francis, 'here is my resignation.'

"The directors reconsidered and rebuilt under Francis' direction. In a year a flood came and the town and the works stood the test. Under the former conditions they would have been swept off the face of the earth. There is a lesson. Learn it."

The influence upon one's life of always expecting and demanding the best effort of one's self cannot be measured. There is a great difference between going just right and a little wrong, — between superiority and mediocrity, — between the fairly good and the best; and there is something in the determination always to keep up the standards in thought, or in whatever we do in life — whether it is hoeing corn, mending shoes, or making laws for a nation — which gives an upward tendency, — an inspiring quality which is lacking in the character of the grovelling man with low ideals. There is something in the upward struggle involved in giving one's best to what he is doing that enlists and develops the highest faculties and calls out the truest and noblest qualities which often lie dormant.

This habit of always doing one's best enters into the very marrow of one's heart and character; it affects one's bearing, one's self-possession. The man who does everything to a finish has a feeling of serenity; he is not easily thrown off his balance; he has nothing to fear, and he can look the world in the face because he feels conscious that he has not put shoddy into anything, that he has nothing to do with shams, and that he has always done his level best. The sense of efficiency, of being master of one's craft, of being equal to any emergency, the consciousness of possessing the ability to do with superiority whatever one undertakes, will give soul-satisfaction which a half-hearted, slipshod worker never knows. The man who has learned the priceless habit of never slighting his work, of always doing to a finish whatever he undertakes, has a perpetual tonic. There is nothing else which gives the satisfaction which comes from a sense of completeness, of wholeness, from an absolutely completed task.

When a man feels throbbing within him the power to do what he undertakes as well as it can possibly be done, and all of his faculties say "Amen" to what he is doing, and give their unqualified approval to his efforts, — this is happiness, this is success. This buoyant sense of power spurs the faculties to their fullest development. It unfolds the mental, the moral, and the physical forces, and this very growth, the consciousness of an expanding mentality and of a broadening horizon, gives an added satisfaction beyond the power of words to describe. It is a realization of nobility, the divinity of the mind.

The writer has a friend who has been of inestimable assistance to him in his work, who has from boyhood made it a rule of his life never to let anything pass out of his hands until it is done to a finish and has received the last touch of his best effort. It does n't matter to him that people are in a hurry, or that others about him are fretting and fuming, — he cannot be induced to slight his work. There must be the stamp of completeness and superiority upon it before he lets it go. During many years of extensive correspondence with him, the writer has not received from him a hurried or slipshod letter or note, or one which was not well balanced and accurately punctuated. People envy this man his superior power to do things, but this is the result of always doing his level best in everything he has touched. He will not guess at a thing, and he insists on absolute accuracy and in doing everything to a complete finish.

The effect of this habit upon this man has been most remarkable; his character is solid and substantial; there is not a false note in his make-up; everything rings true. He is honest, transparent to the very core, and I attribute a large part of this symmetry of character to this life-habit of putting the stamp of superiority upon everything he touches.

While continual and determined thoroughness develops character and leads to success and happiness, one of the greatest success-killers and character-destroyers is a habit of leaving things half done or otherwise incomplete. It makes no difference whether our work is seen or not, for there is a certain something within us which gives approval when a thing is done to a finish, and it says "Right" to a fitting act, or a completed work, and "Wrong" to a half-done job, or a slipshod service. This still, small voice keeps repeating, "Wrong, wrong! You know it is all wrong. It is n't right. You know it is n't right." It tells us that we are failures, and we know when we are failures although the world may applaud us and the press may laud our achievements over the world. A man must learn that there is something greater than the world's applause and nearer and dearer to him than other's approval, — and that is his own. If we cannot have our self-respect the respect of others is only a mockery. However, if lax methods and slipshod works are continued, the self-condemnation wears off, the slack work does not seem such a terrible thing, another temptation to carelessness is yielded to, and soon we are so hardened that some day we are surprised to find that we are habitually slighting work. The tiny departures from conscientiousness have become mighty cables of habit; conscience no longer reproaches; self-respect is no longer outraged. We can do things in the most slipshod manner without the slightest feeling of discomfort or regret. After a while, if the tendency is not checked, the whole character becomes undermined and honeycombed so that everything one does has a certain incompleteness about it, — is not quite right, — lacks something. Such actions affect one's attitude almost as does dishonesty. In fact, it is dishonesty to take a position with the tacit agreement that one will do his level best for his employer and then to slight work, half do it, botch it. Many a criminal, now in prison, could trace his downfall to a habit of half doing things and putting dishonesty into his work.

If you resolutely determine, at the very outset of your career, that you will let no work go out of your hands until it is done just as well as you can do it; that you will put your character into your work, and set upon it the seal of your personal nobility, you will need no other protection, — no patent or copyright. Your work and you will be in demand and, better still, your conscience will be clear, your self-respect firm, and your mind serene and happy.

There never will be a trust in excellence or a combination in superiority. As long as man yearns for improvement and hungers for the larger, the better, the truer, there will always be opportunities. Competition in excellence can never be suppressed as long as man continues to aspire.

XVII.

THE WATCHED BOY.

DID you ever know a boy who was constantly watched and whose every act was scrutinized with severity to amount to anything? Did you ever know a watched boy who did not develop very undesirable qualities? Did you ever know any one who was habitually held under a microscope by a suspicious, exacting parent or teacher to develop a large, broad-minded, magnanimous character? There may be exceptions to the rule in this matter, as in all others, but you will find it true in general that children who are not trusted, and are not put on their honor, will grow into mean, narrow-minded, suspicious men and women.

Like begets like. By a natural law all things seek their affinities. A critical, fault-finding, suspicious nature will awaken and call into action the worst qualities of those with whom it has dealings. Servants of employers of this kind sometimes become dishonest because suspicious thoughts are entertained concerning them so long that they begin to doubt their own integrity, and finally think they may as well have the game as the name. Boys who are conscious of being suspected all the time of doing wrong, of shirking their work, or of slighting their tasks, will come to think, after a while, that they are not worthy of trust and that they must have some bad qualities or parents and teachers would not regard them thus.

If there is one thing more necessary than another to the development of a strong, noble character it is a sense of freedom. A boy must feel that he is trusted, that he is not held under constant suspicion, and that parents and teachers rely upon his honor and believe in his manliness and honesty of purpose, or he will become twisted and distorted from the manner of man that God meant him to be.

You will never get the most or the best your boy is capable of while you watch and distrust him. The very thought that you are watching him makes him self-conscious, destroys his naturalness and spontaneity, and dampens his enthusiasm.

Advise your boy, love him, sympathize with him in his hopes and plans, and show him that you depend upon him to do what is right, and that you trust him absolutely, and you will draw out all that is best and noblest in him. But as long as you repress him, doubt his honesty and honor, and criticise him for every little defection from your idea of what boy should do and be, you will not see him grow into a noble man.

A repressed, enslaved race cannot progress and cannot develop strong character. Neither can a repressed, enslaved individual — man, woman, or child — grow in mental height or breadth.

When the president and professors of Harvard University decided to give each student his liberty, — not to watch him, and not to have him feel that he was under a critical eye all the time, — they were very severely criticised. When they announced that attendance at recitations and chapel exercises would no longer be compulsory, fathers and mothers of Harvard students all over the country threw up their hands in horror, and declared that their boys would go to the dogs. But President Charles W. Eliot thought differently. Observation and experience in his profession had convinced him that the watched student would never develop any desirable character or stamina. He assured the alarmed parents that, in rescinding compulsory rules, he and the other members of the faculty of Harvard were working for the best interests of the students. He pointed out to them that the manhood of their sons must be called out, that they must be trusted to govern and discipline themselves, and that they must be put upon their honor or they would go out from their alma mater, armed with diplomas, it is true, but weaklings in every other respect, — lacking in self-confidence and the power of initiative, and wholly unfitted to cope with the world.

At the time students in all our colleges were watched and hemmed in by cast-iron rules as if they were little children perfectly incapable of self-government. The same was true in our academies and seminaries. Spies were put on the track of the boys and they were run down almost like thieves. They were compelled to attend prayers and chapel exercises and were marked for every absence from recitations or lectures. Rolls were called and they were often induced to lie and give all sorts of excuses for their absences. In short, they were treated as irresponsibles who could not be trusted to regulate their own acts. The result was that, whenever they escaped from under the eyes of the professors, they threw off all restraint and indulged in the wildest excesses. Long repression made them degrade liberty into license whenever they got an opportunity.

CHARLES W. ELIOT.

The reform initiated by Harvard was adopted by the leading educational institutions throughout the country. To-day our best colleges leave their students practically free from all restrictions. They are put upon their manhood, — their honor; they are trusted to govern themselves. They are trained to independence of thought and action, which makes them stronger, more independent, and more orderly men. To-day there is not nearly so large a percentage of arrests or expulsions among Harvard students as before President Eliot introduced his reform, though the institution is very much larger now than it was then.

In order to develop strong independence and individuality there must be liberty of action. It is a thousand times better for a boy to make a mistake now and then, when acting on his own responsibility, than to go always just right while walking on crutches or being led or coerced by some one else. It is better for him to wobble a little when walking alone than to follow an absolutely straight line when being led. It is better for him to acquire self-confidence, even though he must pay for it by suffering defeat, than to be always led by some one else.

XVIII.

THE RIGHT HAND OF GENIUS.

Free men freely work:
Whoever fears God, fears to sit at ease.
ELIZABETH BARRETT BROWNING.

Genuine work alone, what thou workest faithfully, that is eternal as the Almighty Founder and World-Builder. — CARLYLE.

Too busy with the crowded hour to fear to live or die. — EMERSON.

With hand on the spade and heart in the sky,
Dress the ground and till it;
Turn in the little seed, brown and dry,
Turn out the golden millet.
Work and your house shall be duly fed,
Work, and rest shall be won;
I hold that a man would better be dead
Than alive when his work is done.
ALICE CARY.

Thine to work as well as pray,
Clearing thorny wrongs away;
Plucking up the weeds of sin,
Letting heaven's warm sunshine in.
WHITTIER.

"I WORKED all day!" expostulated a French officer, apologizing for not having performed all the work assigned him when the whole army was straining every nerve preparing to invade Egypt.

"But had you not the night also?" asked Napoleon, rebukingly.

Genius, according to the definition of Joshua Reynolds, is "nothing more than the operation of a strong mind accidentally determined as to its object." "When

I hear a young man spoken of as giving promise of high genius," said Ruskin, "the first question I ask about him is, always, 'Does he work?'" Mark these two words, — "operation" and "work." You will find a hundred men to whom that much misapprehended term "genius" has been applied ringing the changes upon *work* as the secret of achievement.

A very foolish notion prevails that the necessity for application is incompatible with great ability. The mistaken idea that the virtues of diligence and industry are inconsistent with marked natural gifts has defeated many a man in the race of life. Youths have the impression that "born genius" will do great things, anyway, and that, if they have genius, they will become great men without exertion. Their ideal of a genius is one who never studies, or who studies nobody can tell when, and now and then strikes off some wonderful production at white heat; a fellow who, occasionally, takes up a pen as a magician's wand to supply his wants, and, when the pressure of necessity is relieved, resorts again to pleasure; an irregular, vagabond sort of person, who muses in the fields or dreams by the fireside; whose strong impulses hurry him into wild irregularities or foolish eccentricities; a man who abhors order and system, who can bear no restraint, and hates detail and labor. They have an idea that success is conquered at a single leap. "A masterly magazine article, a picture dashed off in fiery haste, some speech or deed or stroke of business ability will certainly, ere long, unless they greatly mistake, set the tongues of the town wagging, and carry them straight up the heights." They are waiting and hoping that they may accomplish some great thing in some great emergency, which will attract the attention of the world. They do not realize the power of continued exertion. They have little faith in plodding. They do not understand the magic of industry, the miracle of keeping everlastingly at it.

Have you been accustomed to think of Shakespeare as an ideal of spontaneous genius? Study Ben Jonson's lines about him:

> For, though the poet's matter, nature be,
> His art doth give the fashion. For that, he
> Who casts to write a living line must sweat,
> (Such as thine are) and strike the second heat
> Upon the Muse's anvil; turn the same,
> (And himself with it) that he thinks to frame;
> Or, for the laurel he may gain a scorn, —
> For a good poet's made, as well as born.

Was Lord Byron, do you say, a poet born and not made? Listen to his own words: "The only genius that I know anything of is to work sixteen hours a day."

Did you ever realize what the creation of "David Copperfield," of "Bleak House," or of the "Pickwick Papers" cost Dickens? "My imagination," says he, "would never have served me as it has but for the habit of commonplace, humble, patient, daily toiling, drudging attention."

It required years of drudgery and reading a thousand volumes for George Eliot to get fifty thousand dollars for "Daniel Deronda." Schiller "never could get done." Dante sees himself "growing lean over his 'Divine Comedy.'"

Anthony Trollope, "who never worked for anything but money, and who never for himself, nor anybody else for him, claimed that he possessed genius, although he was a successful novelist, made it a strict duty to write fifteen hundred words a day, rain or shine, in the vein or not in the vein." He followed, if not literally, at least in spirit, the advice which another literary man gave him, and which he gave to Robert Buchanan: "When you sit down to write, put a piece of cobbler's wax on the bottom of your chair! That's the only way to get work done!"

George Parsons Lathrop says that most of the authors whom he has known are obliged to work hard for at least twelve or sixteen hours a day. They are compelled to do this even at times when they would rather rest or sleep, or eat and drink and be merry. "I, myself," says Lathrop, "have often bowed to this necessity of working continuously without sleep or meat or amusement; and should have long since concluded that it must be owing to my own stupidity but for the fact of discovering that other authors, who are much more in the world's eye, have to do the same sort of thing. I love my work, I revere the art which I serve as earnestly as any one can; but, when my fingers have clutched a penholder for eight or ten hours at a stretch, and the whole of such brain and nerve power as I possess has been brought to bear during that time, I confess that a due regard for veracity will not allow me to assert that the process has not involved drudgery. A redeeming and inspiring charm there always is, even in such arduous labors. I have found comfort in toilsome hack work, because it is always satisfactory to perform even obscure service thoroughly and to the best of one's power, and because by such work I could earn time to do higher and better things, which were quite certain not to win for me that cash compensation whereby the mortal part of man is kept going. But, simply on the ground that there is a great and enduring delight in the severest literary exertion, to spread a notion that a professional author need not undergo drudgery seems to me mischievous. It arouses false hopes in young aspirants who have not yet measured the tremendous problem of performing the best work under endless discouragements and at the cost of ceaseless, patient toil."

"I do not remember a book in all the departments of learning," said Beecher, "nor a scrap of literature, nor a work in all the schools of art, from which its author has derived a permanent renown, that is not known to have been long and patiently elaborated. Genius needs industry as much as industry needs genius."

"Genius begins great works," said Joubert; "labor alone finishes them."

"Oh, if I could thus put a dream on canvas!" exclaimed an enthusiastic young artist, pointing to a most beautiful painting. "Dream on canvas!" growled the master, "it is the ten thousand touches with the brush you must learn to put on canvas that make your dream."

After Rubens had become famous and rich an alchemist urged him to assist in transmuting metals into gold, a secret which the scientist felt sure he had discovered. "You have come twenty years too late," replied Rubens; "I discovered the secret long ago." Pointing to his palette and brushes, he added, "Everything I touch turns to gold."

Michael Angelo said of Raphael: "One of the sweetest souls that ever breathed; he owed more to his industry than to his genius."

"Many young painters," asserts Goethe, "would never have taken their pencils in hand if they could have felt, known, and understood, early enough, what really produced a master like Raphael."

"I work harder than any plowman," Millet would sometimes say. "My advice to all boys is 'Work!' They can't all be geniuses, but they can all work; and, without work, even the most brilliant genius will be of very little good. I never recommend any one to be an artist. If a boy has a real calling to be an artist he will be one without being recommended. Scores of people bring their children to me and ask me if I should advise them to bring them up as painters and I always say, 'Certainly not.' But, whatever a boy intends to be, he must grind at it; study all the minutest details and scamp any of the uninteresting elementary part, but be thoroughly well up in all the ground work of the subject."

"Nothing can be done well without taking trouble," said another artist, Alma Tadema. "You must work hard if you mean to succeed."

"People sometimes attribute my success to my genius," said Alexander Hamilton. "All the genius I know anything about is hard work. The genius lies in this: when I have a subject in hand I study it profoundly. Day and night it is before me. I explore it in all its bearings. My mind becomes pervaded with it. Then the effort which I make the people are pleased to call the fruit of genius; it is the fruit of labor and thought."

On his seventieth birthday Daniel Webster told the secret of his success: "Work has made me what I am. I never ate a bit of idle bread in my life."

What said Newton of his accomplishment? "If I have done the public any service it is due to nothing but industry and patient thought."

"A somewhat varied experience of men," says Huxley, "has led me, the longer I live, to set less value on mere cleverness and to attach more and more importance to industry and to physical endurance. No success is worthy of the name unless it is won by honest industry and brave breasting of the waves of fortune."

Turn whichever way you will you will find that, for this man or that who has made himself a name for greatness, the road to distinction has been paved with years of self-denial and hard work, heartaches, headaches, nerveaches, disheartening trials, discouraged hours, fears and despair. It is certain that the greatest poets, orators, statesmen, and historians, men of the most brilliant and imposing talents, have labored as hard, if not harder, than day laborers; and that the most obvious reason why they have been superior to other men is that they have taken more pains than other men. "The infinite capacity for taking pains" is Carlyle's definition of genius. I do not of course say that taking pains will of itself make a genius of you if nature has denied you extraordinary gifts; but I wish to emphasize the fact that it is not the man of the greatest natural vigor and capacity who achieves the highest results, but he who employs his powers with the greatest industry and the most carefully disciplined skill, — the skill that comes by labor, application, and experience. A sound judgment and a close application may do more for you than the most brilliant talent. In the ordinary business of life anything can be done by industry which can be done by "genius;" also many things which "genius," pure and simple, cannot do. There is something for every youth within the reach of industry which "genius" alone can never win. "There is no art or science," says Clarendon, "too difficult for industry to attain to."

"Persevering mediocrity," says one, "is much more respectable and unspeakably more useful than talented inconstancy." "It is not always the highest talent that thrives best," says Joseph Cook; "mediocrity, with tact, will outweigh talent oftentimes." Genius without a sure foundation of common sense and reason, and a very definite knowledge of the importance of work, is of small use to the possessor or to the world. There is probably such a thing as genius; but, nine times out of ten, it is only a great aptitude for patient labor, which is accomplished during the hours when those people born tired by nature are either sleeping, wishing, or hoping that something would turn up, — never exerting themselves to turn up something.

What becomes of the "smart boys" at school who drop back into nothingness so many times when their plodding schoolmates rise slowly but surely? They fall behind in the race of life because they do not feel the need of hard work in their cases; they are impatient of application, irritable, scornful of men's dulness, squeamish at petty disgusts; they love a conspicuous place, short work, and a large reward; they loathe the sweat of toil, the vexations of life, and the dull burden of care.

"There is one precept," said Joshua Reynolds, "in which I shall only be opposed by the vain, the ignorant, and the idle. I am not afraid I shall repeat it too often. You must have no dependence on your own genius. If you have great talents, industry will improve them; if you have but moderate abilities, industry will supply their deficiency. Nothing is denied to well-directed labor; nothing is to be obtained without it."

Worship your heroes if you will; gaze with awe upon the favored of the gods as they tread upon the mountain heights. But remember that it is not alone a sensitive and passionate heart allied to a vivid and powerful imagination that makes your Shakespeare: it is the poet's unceasing toil that "makes" him; his genius appears in his "work" "What men want is not talent, it is purpose; in other words, not the power to achieve, but the will to labor."

XIX.

THE HONEY OF TOIL.

AN ancient Greek thought to save his bees a laborious flight to Hymettus. He cut their wings and gathered flowers for them to work upon at home. But they made no honey; it was the law of their natures to cull from the east and from the west and to bring their sweets from afar.

"We are not sent into this world," says Ruskin, "to do anything into which we cannot put our hearts. We have certain work to do for our bread, and that is to be done strenuously; other work to do for our delight, and that is to be done heartily; neither is to be done by halves or shifts, but with a will; and what is not worth this effort is not to be done at all."

What is it to live? Phillips Brooks answers thus: "The man who knows what it is to act, to work, cries out, 'This, this alone is to live!'"

Nor is it alone because he must work that one who has tasted to the full the cup of labor cries, in exultation, "This alone is to live." "Consider how, even the meanest sorts of service, the soul of man is composed into harmony the instant he sets himself to work. Doubt, desire, sorrow, remorse, indignation, despair itself, lie beleaguering the soul of every man; but, when he bends himself against his task, all these are stilled, and they shrink murmuring far off into their caves. The man becomes a man. The blessed glow of labor in him, is it not as purifying fire!"

"There is one plain rule of life," said John Stuart Mill, " eternally binding and independent of all variations in creeds, embracing equally the greatest moralists and the smallest. It is this: try thyself unweariedly till thou findest the highest thing thou art capable of doing, faculties and outward circumstances being both duly considered, and then do it."

The source of life is closed to him who works not. To be at home in the world, to be at one with all the created world and its Creator, man must do with his might what his hand finds to do; for work is human destiny.

If it be our human destiny even its disagreeable features will be found to have great compensations.

"Our reward is in the race we run, not in the prize."

The wreath of laurel which crowned the victor in the athletic games of old took on its value not in and of itself, but as a symbol of the contest. So does the glory of the reward of our work, however desirable in and of itself, pale beside the glory of the struggle to obtain it. The privilege of running the race with patience is as great as the privilege of wearing the wreath. "See only that thou work," said Emerson, "and thou canst not escape the reward."

"The every day cares and duties which men call drudgery," said Longfellow, " are the weights and counterpoises of the clock of time, giving its pendulum a true vibration and its hands a regular motion; and when they cease to hang upon its wheels, the pendulum no

RALPH WALDO EMERSON.

longer swings, the hands no longer move, the clock stands still."

It is said of Lord Brougham that he was ill at ease if, in the evening, he could not look back upon a faithfully discharged day's work. Duty well performed, he conceived, is the finest conservator, not only of the health of the mind, but also of the health of the body.

A man's business does more to make him than everything else. It hardens his muscles, strengthens his body, quickens his blood, sharpens his mind, corrects his judgment, wakes up his inventive genius, puts his wits to work, starts him on the race of life, arouses his ambition, makes him feel that he is a man and must fill a man's shoes, do a man's work, bear a man's part in life, and show himself a man in that part.

You may leave your millions to your son, but have you really given him anything? You cannot transfer to him the discipline, the experience, the power which the acquisition has given you; you cannot transfer the delight of achieving, the joy felt only in growth, the pride of acquisition, the character which trained habits of accuracy, method, promptness, patience, dispatch, honesty of dealing, and politeness of manner have developed. You cannot transfer the skill, the sagacity, the prudence, the foresight, which lie concealed in your wealth. It meant a great deal for you, but means nothing to your heir. In climbing to your fortune you developed the muscle, the stamina, and the strength which enabled you to maintain your lofty position, to keep your millions intact. You had the power which comes only from experience and which alone enables you to stand firm on your dizzy height. Your fortune was experience to you, joy, growth, discipline, and character; to him it will be a temptation, an anxiety which will probably dwarf him. It was wings to you, but it will be a dead weight to him; it was education to you and expansion of your highest powers, but to him it may mean inaction, lethargy, indolence, weakness, ignorance. You have taken the priceless spur, — necessity, — away from him, the spur which has goaded man to nearly all the great achievements in the history of the world.

You thought it a kindness to deprive yourself in order that your son might begin where you left off. You thought to spare him the drudgery, the hardships, the deprivations, the lack of opportunities, the meagre education which you had. But you have put a crutch into his hand instead of a staff; you have taken away from him the incentive to self-development, to self-elevation, to self-discipline, and self-help, without which no real success, no real happiness, no great character is ever possible. His enthusiasm will evaporate, his energy will be dissipated, and his ambition, not being stimulated by the struggle for self-elevation, will gradually die away. If you do everything for your son except to inculcate habits of work you have left undone the one thing that can preserve him from being a weakling for life.

Labor is the great schoolmaster of the race. It is the grand drill in life's army without which we are only confused and powerless when called into action.

"Work," says Dean Farrar, "is the best birthright which man still retains. It is the strongest of moral tonics, the most vigorous of mental medicines. All nature shows us something analogous to this. The standing pool stagnates into pestilence; the running stream is pure. The very earth we tread on, the very air we breathe, would be unwholesome but for the agitating forces of the wind and sea. In the balmy and enervating regions where the summer of the broad belts of the world furnishes man in prodigal luxuriance with the means of life, he sinks into a despicable and nerveless lassitude; but he is at his noblest and his best in those regions where he has to wrestle with the great forces of nature for his daily bread."

"Thank God every morning when you get up," cried Charles Kingsley, "that you have something to do that day which must be done whether you like it or not. Being forced to work, and forced to do your best, will breed in you temperance, self-control, diligence, strength of will, content, and a hundred other virtues which the idle never know."

What but our hard habits of work, generation after generation, has given stability and meaning to our national life? It has been the salvation of our poorer classes. It has saved thousands of premature deaths, especially by suicide.

"Let a broken man cling to his work," urged Beecher; "if it saves nothing else it will save him."

"How often have I found myself in a state of despondency, with a feeling of depression," exclaimed Professor Virchow, of Berlin. "What has saved me is the habit of work, which has not forsaken me even in the days of outward misfortune, — the habit of scientific work which has always appeared to me as a recreation, even after wearying and useless efforts in political, social, and religious matters."

"Labor is nature's physician," said Galon, the famous Greek physician.

"It is one of the precious compensations of hard work,"

says Matthews, " that there is a *vis medicatrix*, a healing power in it, which is a sovereign remedy for ailments both physical and moral. How often great trials are robbed of their sting by the interest and excitement of an engrossing occupation! But against imaginary grievances, — against hypochondria, low spirits, and *ennui*, — it is a coat of mail. Who, it has been well asked, ever knew a man wretched in his energy? A soldier in the full height of his courage and in the heat of contest is not conscious of a wound. An orator, in the full flow of his 'ignited logic,' is altogether exempt from the pitifulness of rheumatism or the gout. To be occupied — what, indeed, is it? Is it not, literally, to be possessed as by a tenant? When the occupancy is complete, there can be no entrance for any evil spirit. But idleness is emptiness; and, where that is, the doors of the soul are thrown wide open, and the devils of discontent, *ennui* and melancholy troop in, 'not in single spies, but in battalions,' and, once in, they cannot be easily dislodged."

"I have found my greatest happiness in labor," said Gladstone, when nearing four score and ten. "I early formed the habit of industry, and it has been its own reward. The young are apt to think that rest means a cessation from all effort, but I have found the most perfect rest in changing effort. If brain-weary over books and study go out into the blessed sunlight and the pure air and give heartfelt exercise to the body. The brain will soon become calm and rested. The efforts of nature are ceaseless. Even in our sleep the heart throbs on. If these great forces ceased for an instant, death would follow. I try to live close to nature and to imitate her in my labors. The compensation is sound sleep, a wholesome digestion, and powers that are kept at their best; and this, I take it, is the chief reward of industry."

Bismarck urged hard work as the only safeguard for a true life. A few years before his death, when asked for a rule of life which would be simply stated and easily recommended, he said: "There is one word which expresses this rule, this gospel, — work; without work, life is empty, useless, and unhappy. No man can be happy who does not work. To the youth on the threshold of life I have not one word, but three words of advice to offer, — ' work, work, work!' "

"Labor is everlastingly noble and holy," says Carlyle; "it is the source of all perfection; no man can accomplish, or become accomplished, without work; it is the purifying fire burning up the poisoning and corrupting influences emasculating the manhood of the soul." "Work is the grand cure for all maladies and miseries that ever beset mankind," continues the sage of Chelsea. "There is a perennial nobleness and even sacredness in work. Were he never so benighted, forgetful of his high calling, there is always hope in a man who honestly and earnestly works; in idleness alone is there perpetual despair." "All true work is sacred; in all true work, were it but true hand labor, there is something of divineness. Labor, wide as the earth, has its summit in heaven." "Work is worship! He that understands this well understands the prophecy of the whole future; it is the last evangel, which has included all others." "Two men I honor, and no third. First, the toil-worn craftsman, that with earth-made implement laboriously conquers the earth and makes her man's. Venerable to me is the hard hand. A second man I honor, and still more highly; him who is seen toiling for the spiritually indispensable; not daily bread, but the Bread of Life. If the poor and humble toil that we may have food must not the high and glorious toil for him in return that we have light, have guidance, freedom, immortality? These two in all their degrees I honor; all else is chaff and dust."

DR. FARRAR IN MIDDLE LIFE.

XX.

THE ELEMENT WHICH DISTINGUISHES WORK FROM DRUDGERY.

THERE is an infinite difference between the manner in which two people do the same thing. We know women who make an art of housekeeping. It does not matter whether they are making bread, pies, dressing a bed, or dusting furniture, they do it with the air of artists. They take a delight in doing what other women seem to hate. To them there is no drudgery in taking care of children or of the house. They lift everything into the artistic realm. In fact, we know women who do the commonest duties with such dignity, and carry themselves with such serenity and ease that it is a real pleasure to watch them about their work. They take a delight in arranging every piece of furniture and every bit of bric-a-brac so that it will express taste. The whole atmosphere of the home is that of refinement, fitness. There is something about it which satisfies the mind.

We know other women who seem to look upon every bit of work about the house as drudgery, to be gotten rid of if possible. They dread the work. They postpone it as long as they can and then rush it anyway to get through with it, and after they are done there is not the slightest sense of harmony or fitness about the house. Nothing satisfies the mind. You have a feeling that everything is at sixes and sevens. In other words, the work has been done in the spirit of the artisan, while the other woman did hers with the spirit of an artist.

You can tell very quickly when one likes his work. There is a creative quality in it, a spontaneity, a delicacy of touch and of treatment, a naturalness which is never found in work that is looked upon as drudgery.

Some women become cross and crabbed if a servant happens to be sick or away and they have to take her place; while other women are gracious and sympathetic and seem only too glad to give the hired girl an occasional holiday, even when others would not, and seem to take a delight in preparing the meal and doing the work themselves. In other words, one does her work gladly, cheerfully, artistically, — she puts her soul into it, expresses her taste, and gives it a touch of refinement and delicacy, — while the other's work is done just the reverse.

We see the same thing in the office, the store, and the factory. Some employees drag themselves around as though it were a real burden to exist, giving you the impression all the time that they hate their work and they wish it were over, that they do not see why they have to do such drudgery while others have easier positions. It tires one to see these employees make such hard work of everything, — everything they take hold of they seem to despise, — while it is a real delight to manage and to have around one employees who go to their work with a light, glad heart, who are always cheerful, optimistic, helpful, always wanting to do something for you, anxious to see your business prosper. There is a great difference between the whole-hearted and half-hearted work, between enthusiastic and lukewarm service, between the dead-in-earnest worker and the indifferent one.

Every manager and proprietor instinctively feels the helpfulness of the conscientious, the glad, willing, earnest worker. He feels an uplift which is a great encouragement to him. These employees radiate a helpfulness which he feels constantly. He knows what employees are trying to help him and those who are shirking and who are afraid they will earn a cent more than is found in their pay envelope.

On the other hand he feels the depression, the dragging, discouraged, don't care spirit, which the indifferent, careless, lazy employees radiate. You feel instinctively drawn towards those who work in the right spirit and are interested in your welfare, and you have a repulsive feeling when you come near those who do not care what becomes of your business if they can only shirk their responsibility and work.

We know shoemakers, men who will sew a patch on a shoe or put on a sole so neatly, and do it so daintily, delicately, and artistically that you feel that they are real artists, that they put their heart into their work, while other shoemakers will put on patches as though they did it just for a living and did not care how they looked. The first seemed to do the work because they liked it, and did not think of what they were going to get out of it, but were anxious to make the neatest looking job of any shoemaker in town.

We know stenographers who do their work so accurately and cheerfully that it gives an employer real pleasure. We know others who are so slovenly about their work, so indifferent and careless, — it never seems to trouble them because they have made a mistake, —

that they are a constant anxiety, while the former seem to feel as pained at a mistake or if they cause their employer anxiety or loss as though the business was their own.

We know teachers who go to their school as a great master would go to his canvas, — with the whole heart throbbing with helpfulness and with sympathy and a dead-in-earnest desire to be of real help to the pupils. They seem to try to radiate sunshine and helpfulness from every pore. The schoolroom seems to be their studio. They are masters in their line. Their whole heart is in their work. Other teachers start off in the morning feeling that it is a bore to go and try to teach those stupid children, and they wish they were not obliged to do it. They put no enthusiasm, they infuse no life or heart into their teaching. This spirit, of course, is contagious and the scholars, of course, take no interest, except now and then one who would be a scholar anyway.

The same thing is true of the clergymen. One will go into the pulpit as Michael Angelo would go to his block of marble which he kept by the side of his bed so that he could go to his loved work as soon as the day dawned. They look upon their work as a great privilege, as a perpetual delight. They do it in the spirit of an artist, while other clergymen seem to be indifferent of the welfare of their flocks. They love to read, perhaps, or enjoy social life, but they do not carry that zest and enthusiasm, that dead-in-earnestness, that desire to help and to inspire that the great master carries into his work.

It is this artistic quality, this soul spirit, this dead-in-earnestness which distinguishes the work of an artist from the work of a drudge.

It is a great thing to form the habit of infusing the spirit of the artist into everything we do.

We knew a man in Rhode Island who built a stone wall with the same spirit that a great artist would paint his masterpiece. He would turn every stone over and study its character and try to place it to the best possible advantage, and after he had built a rod of wall he would stand off and look at it from every possible angle with the same satisfaction that a great sculptor would look at the statue which he had called out of the marble. He put his character, his enthusiasm in every stone he laid. Wealthy summer visitors often went to call upon this farmer, who built even a stone wall in the spirit of an artist, and he loved to tell them about the individuality and the character of the stones and how he managed to make them express themselves to the best advantage, and what it meant to build a piece of wall so that it would stand for a century.

XXI.

THE HABIT OF NOT FEELING WELL.

The outer is always the shadow and form of the inner. — MOZOOMDAR.

GOETHE stated an important truth when he said: "All men would live long, but no man would grow old." Every normal human being desires health, — beauty, — life, in all its joy and fulness. The realization of such desires would effectually prevent us from growing old, no matter how the years might be counted.

Is it possible for us to actualize here and now what we so ardently long for? If it were not, the longing would not be so strongly implanted in us. If we accept this conclusion we must go a step farther and acknowledge that the conditions we desire are under our own control.

Few people realize that their ailments are largely self-induced. They get into a habit of not feeling well. If they rise in the morning with a slight headache or some other trifling indisposition, instead of trying to mount above this condition they take a positive pleasure in expatiating upon their feelings to any one who will listen. Instead of combating the tendency to illness by filling the lungs with pure, fresh air, they dose themselves with "headache tablets" or some other patent specific warranted to cure whatever ill they think they are suffering from. They begin to pity themselves and

GOETHE.

try to attract pity and sympathy from others. Unconsciously, by detailing and dwelling upon their symptoms, they reënforce the first simple suggestions of illness by a whole army of thoughts and fears and images of disease, until they are unfitted to do a day's work in their homes or offices.

It is said that man is a lazy animal. We are all more or less prone to indolence and it is the easiest and most natural thing in the world for young people to accustom themselves to lying down or lounging on a sofa because they think they are tired or not well. Much of the so-called invalidism is simply laziness fostered and indulged from childhood.

There is great danger that young girls who are delicate while growing up, and lounge around the house and lie down whenever they feel the least bit out of sorts, will form a habit of invalidism when they reach maturity.

How often do we see such girls "brace up" at once when anything happens which interests or excites them! An invitation to a reception or a ball, or any other pleasant social function, acts like a tonic. For the time being an instantaneous cure is effected. They are as well as anybody until after the entertainment.

Indulgent mothers are frequently to blame for this physical and mental laziness — for it is nothing more — on the part of their daughters. A lounge or sofa is a positive curse in many a house, because it is such a temptation to lie down and succumb to trifling suggestions of illness or the least indisposition. A habit of giving in whenever you "don't feel like it" is fatal to all achievement and ruinous to self-discipline, self-poise, and nobility and dignity of bearing.

When some one asked a noted opera singer if she was

ever sick and unable to fill her engagements, she replied: "No, we singers cannot afford to be sick. We must fill our engagements; we are not rich enough to give up."

Actors and actresses, as well as singers, are compelled by the necessities of their profession to set aside personal feelings and keep faith with the public, no matter whether they are well or not. They simply cannot spare themselves even when they are really sick, not to speak of giving way to moods or fancied ailments. What would become of their reputations, their careers, if they should fail to appear in public every time they "don't feel like it"?

What is the result of this compulsion upon actors and singers to conquer moods and feelings? Is it not well known that, in spite of the exacting nature of their duties, the late hours they are obliged to keep, the constant wear on the mental and physical faculties, if they take proper care of their health, they retain youth and vitality to a far more advanced age than men and women in other callings? Joseph Jefferson, Denman Thompson, Adelina Patti, Sarah Bernhardt, and many others of the past and present might be cited as examples.

The body is like an easy-going horse that will become lazy and jog along in an indolent, slouching gait if not kept up to "standards" and "style" by its coachman. If the mind, the driver of the body, lets the reins hang loose and allows the body to follow its inclinations, standards will soon be lowered.

No one feels "up to concert pitch" all the time, and it is necessary to train one's self to keep at his task whether he likes it or not.

What if the business man who is compelled to work all day, and who has neither time nor opportunity to coddle himself whether he feels well or not, should become the slave of whims and fancies? Supposing he should say to himself, "I am liable to be ill this summer so I am going to prepare for the worst. I shall have a couch put into my office so that I can lie down when I feel seedy, and I'll lay in a stock of medicine so as to be ready for any emergency." A common-sense business man would consider it a disgrace to even think of such a thing. He knows perfectly well that if he were to act in that way his business would soon "go to the dogs." He knows, also, from experience that it is not necessary to give up every time he "don't feel like it."

Suppose that a general should find his soldiers lounging about the camp, lying under the trees and taking it easy, and many of them not feeling like drilling and should decide to wait until they should all feel like it. What kind of an army would he have? What kind of discipline? The men must fall into line and commence the drill on the appointed minute whether they feel like it or not; if they are positively sick, they must go to the hospital; but they must either be in the hospital, sick enough to be under a doctor's care, or they must drill.

The world is a camp. We are all soldiers under the command of a Supreme General who expects us to be on drill every day unless we are actually disabled.

The moment you allow yourself to be governed by your moods and fancies you open the door to a host of enemies to your health, success, and happiness. Don't under any circumstances sympathize with sick, diseased, or lazy thoughts. If you once yield to such thoughts before you know it you may be their slave.

Some people actually attract illness to themselves by constantly thinking about it. They feel sure that if they should happen to get their feet wet they would soon be sick with pneumonia or influenza. If they happen to be in a draught for a few minutes they are confident that dire results will follow. They will have chills or sore throat. If they cough a little they have dreadful visions of consumption. Is it not in the family? They thus fix images of sickness in the mind and so lessen its power of resistance to disease and make the body more susceptible to the very things they fear.

A conviction that we should be master of ourselves under all conditions would protect us from many of the ills to which we fall easy victims. If we think diseased thoughts, we attract disease. If we think healthy thoughts, we attract health.

The best safeguard you can throw around yourself is a determination that you will be master of yourself, — that you will not be dictated to by moods or whims or fancies of any kind. You will find that if you expect great things of yourself, if you always exact a high standard and accept no apologies or excuses from Mr. Liver, Mr. Stomach, Mr. Nerve, or Mr. Head, your health will be better and you will accomplish infinitely more than if you allow your feelings to hold you in subjection.

It does not take a great deal of practice to be able to throw off any ordinary symptom of indisposition by holding firmly in the mind the opposite thought, — health and cheerfulness. Insist that you will not give up; and that you will do your day's work to the best of your ability, and it is probable that, before the day is half done, you will feel better. This is not theoretical; it is scientific.

We all know people who have fallen into a habit of never feeling well. No matter how soundly they sleep, how good their appetites, or how healthy they appear to be, every inquiry in regard to their condition receives the same stereotyped, depressing answer conveyed in a dismal voice, — "Not very well," "About the same," or "Not so well." These are the people who "enjoy poor health." The only subject of conversation in which they take any interest is themselves. They never weary of discussing their symptoms. They will dilate by the hour on the attack of indigestion, the peculiar sensations which they feel in their heads, stomachs, or backs, or the shooting pains in various parts of their bodies.

Like sailors who tell their "yarns" so often that they really come to believe them themselves, these people dwell so persistently on their fancied or merely temporary petty ailments that they take it for granted that all their imaginings about themselves must be true.

The ailing habit is especially active during spring and summer. When the weather changes and the temperature becomes more variable, the chronic ailers take it for granted that they are not going to feel so well, and so they prepare mentally and physically for the worst. The moment they experience the slightest debility from the warm weather they begin to try new remedies and to complain more than ever before; and the more they coddle themselves and the more they complain the less they feel like doing anything. All day long they lounge on sofas or recline in easy chairs. The mind sympathizes with the posture of the body; the recumbent or lolling attitude quickly reacts upon the mentality, and standards all drop.

If you ever expect to amount to anything in the world you should resist an inclination to loll or lounge around as you would a temptation to any other evil tendency. You can never make the most of yourself if you succumb to the lounging habit. It is so insidious that, almost before you are aware of it, it will sap your ambition and lessen your chances of success. Compel yourself to get up, to brace up, and to keep up to your proper standard whether you feel like it or not.

Have no fellowship with slouchy, slipshod, "don't feel like it" moods. Drive them all away from you as you would drive a thief from your house.

How can you expect to be healthy and robust physically and mentally when you are half the time in a lazy, horizontal attitude? Until you arouse yourself and act as if you were a vertebrate animal you will be neither healthy nor successful. You cannot accomplish good work until you put yourself in the attitude of achievement. You cannot have confidence in your ability to do things while your mental and physical standards are low.

Self-confidence has a great deal to do with one's health.

If, for instance, you have anything of importance to do, and if failure to do it would mean a great loss to you, you would not allow any ordinary feeling of indisposition to prevent its accomplishment. The conviction that you must do a thing, the belief that you can and your determination to do it at all hazards have a great deal to do with the suppression of mental or physical discords.

The influence of expecting yourself to do a good day's work and demanding it of yourself works like magic. It is a powerful tonic.

THE HABIT OF NOT FEELING WELL. 129

Remember that your resisting power, that innate force which was given you for self-protection, is your safeguard not only against mental but also against physical ills.

The moment a fighting general and his army give up they are beaten. The moment your will capitulates, — the moment you admit to yourself that you are going to be captured by the enemy, — you have laid down your arms and virtually surrendered.

A habit of asserting stoutly and defiantly your determination to do a good day's work every day of your life, unless positively sick, will accomplish more for you than all the sanitariums in the world.

How many, who were really life-long invalids, seldom free from bodily suffering, have achieved remarkable success! Charles Darwin, Elizabeth Barrett Browning, Herbert Spencer, Robert Louis Stevenson, Dr. Samuel Johnson, Dr. Kane, the explorer, and many others, more or less eminent, conquered real physical ills in order to pursue their work. If those people had waited for a favorable mood until they felt like it, they would probably never have accomplished anything of note. If the men and women who have pushed civilization up from savagery had dropped their work every time they "did not feel like it," where would the world be to-day?

This matter of feeling well or ill, or of working or not working, is largely a question of mental dominion.

The writer knows a physician's wife, a very estimable lady, who has been subject for years to occasional severe attacks of headache which last for three or four days. While these attacks last she is completely prostrated. She says, however, that, when anything of supreme importance makes it imperative that she should fulfil the duties of her position, she is always able to postpone an attack, sometimes for days at a time.

Now, if any one can postpone a sick headache or other ailment for days at a time in order to attend some special function, is it not reasonable to suppose that it could be postponed indefinitely?

When Douglas Jerrold was told by his physician that he must die, he replied: "What, and leave a family of helpless children? *I won't die.*" His resolution helped him over the crisis, and he lived many years longer. The way to be well is to think health-thoughts.

Determine that you will have nothing to do with abnormities of any kind. Resolve that you will keep yourself up to a high standard mentally, morally, and physically and that you will always be ready to take hold of the duty which lies nearest with vigor and determination.

Do not allow yourself to get into the way of staying at home whenever you do not feel like going to your office, store, or place of business. Oftentimes, especially during summer, the temptation is very strong in the morning, when one feels languid or lazy from the heat, to say to one's self, "Well, I don't feel like it to-day. I think I shall take it easy and let things take care of themselves until I am up to the mark." Now this is just the encouragement the lazy body wants, and you cannot afford to let the temptation conquer you. You must always be master of the situation, and, when your faculties and functions are like soldiers who do not care to drill, but whose duty is to do so, you must assume the office of commanding general.

Don't allow yourself to become a slave to the miserable

little absorbers of your health and happiness. Every time a diseased thought, a thought inimical to your health or achievement comes to you, expel it at once. Don't stop to discuss, or weigh, or consider it. Drive it off if it is not a friend and replace it by a strong, healthy, beautiful thought. If you persist in this course you will fill your mind with hosts of health thoughts, beauty thoughts, and achievement thoughts which will make you physically and mentally vigorous, successful, and happy.

XXII.

KEEPING FIT FOR WORK.

"A GREAT electric power-plant with half its dynamos out of commission through short-circuits and burn-outs caused by overloads, and several at half-speed, with wobbling bearings and loosened bolts, — that is what half the men and workers are like. They are not using half their power, half their talents, half their physiques, half their minds." Very few people bring the whole of themselves to their task. The causes are various — systemless working, vicious living, wrong thinking, wrong methods, wrong occupations.

The real material with which you build your career is in you. Your own self is your greatest capital. The secret of your future achievement is locked up in your brain, in your nerves, in your muscles, in your ambition, in your determination, and in your ideal. Everything depends upon your physical and mental condition, for that governs your vitality, your vigor, and your ability to do things. The amount of physical and mental force you are able to use in your vocation will measure your ultimate success, and whatever lessens this force, or the effectiveness of your achievement capital, will cut down your usefulness in life and your chances of success. Achievement does not depend so much upon the size of the deposits you have in the bank as upon the amount of capital you have in yourself, the effectiveness with which you can use it, and the power you can bring to your vocation. A man who is weakened by ill health, or who has sapped his energy by excessive use of tobacco or alcohol, or in any other way, has small chance for success when pitted against one who is sound and vigorous in every organ and faculty.

Nature is not sentimental or merciful. If you violate her law you must pay the penalty, though you sit on a throne; king or beggar is all the same with her. You cannot plead weakness or handicap as an excuse for failure. She demands that you be ever at the top of your condition, that you always do your best, and will accept no excuse or apology.

A weakness anywhere mars one's whole career. It will rise up as a ghost all through one's life-work, mortifying, condemning, and convicting one of past error. Every indiscretion or vicious indulgence simply opens a leak which drains off success capital.

Of what use is great success capital, of mental and physical equipment, if you are not wise enough to manage it to the best advantage, and to make it last until your success is assured?

It is sad to see a young man try to win high place with a broken-down constitution, or with his faculties half trained, and his success army completely demoralized, his prospects ruined by a shattered physique. The saddest think of all is that wise living might have made fulfilment of ambition possible and enriched the world with a noble, well-rounded life.

The great problem, then, which every one has to face, is how to generate energy, how to conserve it, and how to keep one's self always at the top of his condition.

If you are level-headed, dead in earnest, and bound to make the most of yourself, you will regard every bit of energy, and every source of power, physical, mental, and moral, as precious life capital not to be parted with except for some worthy equivalent. You will look upon every form of dissipation and every little loss of energy as an unpardonable waste, a sin, — almost a crime. You will stop every leak of energy and prevent every unnecessary drain of your success capital, so that all the force you can muster, all the power you can command, shall be expanded most economically and effectively. You will keep every faculty and function up to a standard of the highest excellence so that you can come to your task in the morning a whole man, with every faculty intent, and every function normal. If you cannot carry a strong vigorous personality to your work every day, or if you bring but a small part of yourself to your task, you will realize but a small part of your possibilities.

One of the most foolish or insane things that a person can do is to go to his work in the morning with vitiated energy, wasted vitality, and a system so wearied that he cannot do vigorous, spontaneous work, but must force himself to do everything by sheer will power.

Keep yourself fit for work, so that you can do it with ease and dignity, and without struggle, strain, or loss. Approach your work with the air of a conqueror, and with assurance of victory in your very step. If you are at the top of your condition, your manner, even, will radiate power. You will exhale force from every pore. One can accomplish more in a single hour, if he feels the thrill of health pulsating through his entire being, than he can in a whole day if his physical condition is at a low ebb.

There is no success in weakness, no victory in the uncertain step, hesitating will, lagging hand, or languid brain of an exhausted man. He who is hampered by depleted vitality is constantly losing opportunities, because he lacks strength to grasp them, to hold on to them, and to use them. He is forced to fall behind and see men who have not half his mental capacity, but who have strong physiques and all their power intact, forge ahead of him and seize the prizes.

A great many people dissipate more energy between the time when they leave their work at night and when they return to it in the morning than they expend all day on their vocations, though they would be shocked and offended if any one were to tell them so. They think that physical dissipation is the only method of energy-sapping. But men and women of exemplary moral habits dissipate their vitality in a hundred ways. They indulge in wrong thinking; they worry; they fret; they fear this, that, and the other imaginary thing; and they carry their business home with them, and work as hard mentally after business hours as during them.

Whenever you are angry or feel like grumbling, or pouting, — whenever you are gloomy, fretful, or morose, — you are consuming your energy, wasting your vitality, and opening the sluice-ways in your mental reservoir, instead of sending the power over the wheel to drive the mental machinery.

Thackeray says, "Every man has a letter of credit written on his face." We are our own best advertisements, and if we appear to disadvantage in any particular, our standard, in the estimate of others, is cut down. The great majority of people who come in contact with us do not see us at our homes; they may never see our stocks and bonds, or lands and houses; they know nothing of us, unless it be by reputation, but what they see of our personality, and they judge us accordingly. They take it for granted that our general appearance is a sample of what we are and what we can do, and, if we are slovenly in dress, and in personal habits, they naturally think that our work and our lives will correspond. They are right. It does not matter where the slackness or shiftlessness manifests itself, or what its nature may be, it will reappear in your work, in your manner, and in your person. Many people form a careless habit of neglecting some part of their toilet, as when they black only the front part of their shoes and leave the heels untouched. The same incompleteness, the same lack of finish will appear in every letter they write and in every piece of work they attempt to do. It will prove a detriment to character-growth. The consciousness of incompleteness, or "slipshodness," tends to destroy self-respect, to lessen energy, and to detract from one's general ability.

In these days of inexpensive clothing no one can afford to leave his room until he is in a condition to be presentable anywhere. Neither can he afford to bother about thinking of his clothing after he is once dressed, but he should so clothe himself that he will be utterly unconscious of any inferiority. A sense of being fittingly and appropriately dressed increases one's efficiency and self-respect, and so adds materially to achievement. If you are improperly dressed or badly "groomed" you will feel a certain timidity in meeting people, a loss of power. This results in uneasiness, worry, chagrin, and a real loss of energy and self-confidence.

Girls who are not obliged to leave home to earn their living have a much weaker incentive to keep themselves up to standard than young men. If at all indolent they are often tempted to lie abed late, or to lounge around the house in slipshod apparel. Under such conditions many a girl falls into careless ways and deteriorates mentally and physically, developing an aversion to anything active or strenuous. Letting down all standards she slides along, listless, indifferent, and useless.

A young man, on the contrary, who knows that he must get up at a certain hour, and that he must be neatly dressed and in his place, ready to begin his day's work at an appointed time, or else lose his position, must perforce "keep up to concert pitch." He does not have a chance to consult his moods or to ask himself whether he feels like getting up and going out or not. He knows very well that he has no choice.

A young man who is trying to make the most out of his life cannot be too good to himself. Everything which ministers to his comfort and ease gives him a sense of harmony, assurance, and added power. Anything which will add to his self-respect, and will keep discord away from him, he should have at any cost he can afford.

Above all else, he should have a cozy, comfortable, and happy home. No man can do good work when he goes every night to an unattractive, uncomfortable, or discouraging home. He should provide himself with a good light, and an easy chair; he should surround himself with pictures and other works of art if possible. Every one should have a comfortable sitting room, or a cozy corner somewhere, where he can read, think, and reflect by himself, — then he will grow. A great many boys and young men are totally unfitted for doing good work, especially in the evening, because they do not have an attractive place which tempts them to self-improvement.

A habit of keeping up to concert pitch and maintaining a high standard all along the line is of untold advantage.

XXIII.

THE POWDER OF SUCCESS.

"ENERGY is what wins. Many men fail to reach the mark because the powder in them is not proportioned to the bullet."

More men fail of success in life from lack of energy — that force which achieves, accomplishes, pushes its way through obstacles — than from almost anything else. No matter how much ability a young man may have, or how clever, courteous, or amiable he may be, if he lacks energy, the powder of success, he never will accomplish much.

Nothing else, excepting honesty, is so much in demand in these days as "vim." Everybody believes in it; everywhere we hear: "Give us a man who can *do* something; a man who has push; a man with iron in his blood." Ability is worthless without the power to put it into action. Resolutions, however good, are useless without the energy necessary to carry them out. Push clears the track; people get out of the way of an energetic man. Even small ability with great energy will accomplish more than the greatest ability without energy. If fired from a gun with sufficient velocity a tallow candle can be shot through an inch board.

On every hand we see fine young men and women failing, their ability going to waste, standing in equilibrium, for the lack of "force." If we could only shake them up, put a little powder into them and set them going, they might amount to something, but without this they are failures. They seem to have every other quality except that power of pushing their way, without which almost all their ability is wasted. The finest engine ever made would be absolutely useless without power to propel it and drag the load to its destination.

The world admires energetic men. Blow them this way and that, and they only bend; they never break. Put obstacles in their way, and they surmount them. It is almost impossible to keep such men down. Trip one up, and instantly he is on his feet again; bury him in the mud and almost instantly he is up and at it again. Such men as he build cities, establish schools and hospitals, whiten the ocean with sails, and blacken the air with the smoke of their industry.

The pathway of life is strewn with wrecks of those who have failed because they lacked this propelling power. The moment they strike an obstacle, they stop; they have no power to climb or overcome. The genius of achievement seems to have been left out of their makeup; their blood lacks the iron of energy, the force of accomplishment.

Nature has stored in every normal youth a reservoir of physical and mental energy which means much in the way of character, success, and happiness. The word economy is usually applied to the saving of money, but this, perhaps, is the least important of its applications. Wasting money is of little importance when compared with wasting energy, mental and vital forces and opportunities, a waste that endangers our highest welfare.

Many a man who is economical to stinginess in money matters squanders, with fearful waste, his mental and moral energy. It is considered a terrible thing for a youth to spend a thousand dollars of his father's money in a single night's dissipation; but what about the strain upon his vitality, the life forces which he throws away, or the wasted energy which might have been put into physical and mental achievement? What is the loss of money compared with the demoralization wrought by such a debauch? What are a thousand dollars in comparison with even a small fraction of precious life-power? Money lost may be regained, but vitality lost in dissipation not only cannot be regained, but it is also a thousand times worse than lost, because it has demoralized all that is left, deteriorated the character, and undermined the very foundation of all that is best in life.

Many busy people are shameful wasters of time and opportunity, simply because they do low things when higher ones are possible. They read a poor book when they might read a better one. They squander time with bad companions when good ones are possible. They waste time in half-doing things, in botching, bungling and blundering, in doing things over and over because they were not done right the first time.

A great waste of mental and moral vitality is indulging in demoralizing, vicious and deteriorating thoughts. Every bit of useless worry, — and all worry is useless, — every bit of anxiety, every particle of fretting and stewing, every bit of despondency, indulgence in melancholy or foreboding, every bit of fear, — fear of failure, of losses, of sickness, of disease, of death, of unjust criticism or ridicule, or of the unfavorable opinions of others,

— all these things are vitality-sappers, worse than useless, for they unfit us for constructive, creative work by squandering that which makes such work possible.

One is wasting life force every time he talks of failure, of hard luck, of troubles and trials, of past errors and mistakes. If one would succeed, let him turn his back on the past, burning all the bridges behind him; turn his back to shadows and face the light. Every act of dishonesty, whether others know it or not, is a terrible life-waster. Every act or thought of impurity, every unholy desire, is a virtue-waster, a success-sapper.

Everything which frets, chafes, rasps or brings inharmony into life is a vitality-waster. Whatever brings discord into the nervous system destroys power. Friction is a deadly foe to happiness and success. It grinds away the delicate bearings of life's machinery without doing any good work or increasing any value. To free life from friction, to lubricate all the faculties, and to stop all the leaks of energy, is the first duty to one's self and to others.

Everywhere we go we see human machines going rattlety bang, clattering and thumping, grinding the bearings of the delicate human machinery, creaking from the lack of oil, bearings hot and hissing from leaks of the steam-valves. This delicate, living, pulsating machinery is filled with the dust of worry, the delicate bearings being scratched with anxiety. Everywhere we see frightful waste of energy — force oozing out of the holes of carelessness, of dissipation in the boiler. This wonderful machinery, so marvelously constructed, so delicately adjusted, and intended for running at least a century, we find thrown aside on the scrap pile before the owner has reached middle life. How careful he has been of his chronometer to wind it at just such a time, to have it cleaned regularly and adjusted and regulated to a fraction of a second a month ; and yet, his living machine of infinite value, and which he cannot by any possibility duplicate, he abuses every day of his life. He would not think of exposing the works of his delicate watch to the damp air, or carrying it near the electric dynamo, and yet he abuses his living machine in all sorts of ways. By fits of jealousy, of hot temper, by hatred and by frightful dissipation, he racks and wrenches and warps this intricate, delicate, throbbing piece of mechanism — exposes it to all sorts of indignities — until it is no longer capable of running without jar, until it rattles and shakes and trembles and wobbles itself into a perfect wreck before it has accomplished a tithe of its work or served its purpose.

XXIV.

MASTERING MOODS.

PASCAL says that "the whole dignity of man is in thought," and that "his whole duty is to think correctly." This is a sweeping statement, and yet every word or act of ours is simply the expression of a thought. Unless we learn to think correctly, therefore, life must be a failure. Instead of being the dignified, happy, and beautiful thing that the Creator meant it to be, it will be mean, unhappy, unlovely and unsuccessful.

The very first condition necessary to make life yield all its possibilities is health, — that abounding vitality and vigor of mind and body which make living joyous, — and health is dependent upon correct thought. Every function, every nerve cell, every organ in the body is powerfully influenced by the nature of our thoughts. There is no more firmly established scientific principle than that we experience the reaction of our thoughts, either in increased strength and vitality, or the opposite.

To have a perfectly healthy body, one must possess a cheerful, healthy, optimistic mind. Love, peace, joy, gladness, kindness, unselfishness, contentment, serenity, — these are the mental attributes which, by bringing all the bodily functions into harmony, produce a sound, healthy body. Any one who chooses may externalize these attributes in himself by persistent, correct thinking.

"I have seen gleams in the face and eyes of the man," says Carlyle, "that have let you look into a higher country." It is in that "higher country" that we must live continually if we would dominate our moods and attain that peace and serenity which insure health and happiness. It is not an easy matter to conquer wrong thinking. Captious moods, fretfulness, worry, anxiety, fear — all the little imps of the mind that perpetually seek to draw us from the higher to the lower country — can only be overcome by constant watchfulness and the greatest earnestness and persistence.

Wrong thinking is indicative of weakness; it is, indeed, a species of insanity, for a wrong thinker is continually tearing down and wrecking his own mental and physical structure. The right thinker is the only sane thinker, and he is the happiest as well as the most successful man. He knows better than to keep constantly tripping himself up with the adverse thought which produces destructive conditions.

We all know the disastrous effects of wrong thinking. We know by experience how it cripples us mentally and physically. Physicians are well aware that anger poisons the blood, and that fear, anxiety, fretting, and all other inharmonious thoughts seriously interfere with the normal action of all the bodily functions. They are also alive to the fact that anxiety or apprehension of impending disaster, if of long duration, is liable to bring on paralysis. It is an established fact that a mother is not only seriously affected by her own thought, but that it affects her infant to such an extent that the same symptoms and conditions from which the mother suffers are reproduced in the body of the infant. Selfishness, jealousy, and envy long indulged in tend to produce serious liver troubles and certain forms of dyspepsia. Lack of self-control and habitual indulgence in violent passions shatter the nervous system, lessen the will power, and induce grave disorders. Worry is one of the greatest enemies of the human race; it carves its deep furrows wherever it goes; it carries gloom and unhappiness with it; it delays or prevents the processes of digestion and assimilation until the starved brain and nerve cells utter their protest in various kinds of disease, sometimes even in insanity.

Wrong thinking, whatever its nature, leaves indelible scars on mind and body alike. It affects character and material prospects equally. Every time you grumble or find fault; every time you lose your temper; every time you do a mean contemptible thing, you suffer a loss which cannot be repaired. You lose a certain amount of power, of self-respect, and of an uplifting and up-building character-force. You are conscious of your loss, too, which tends to weaken you still further.

A business man will find that, every time he gets out of sorts, flies into a rage, or "goes all to pieces" when things go wrong, he is not only seriously injuring his health, but is also crippling his business. He is making himself repellent; he is driving away success conditions.

A man who wants to do his best must keep himself in good mental trim. If he would achieve the highest success he must be a correct thinker. He cannot think discord and bring harmonious conditions into his business. His wrong thought will honeycomb and undermine his prospects in life.

Many a once prosperous man has gone down in financial ruin because he had not learned how to control his thoughts. He gave way to the "blues;" he began to worry and fret and find fault with everybody. The fault-finding habit became fixed and continued until he sank into a condition where nothing suited him and nobody could please him. His old employees left him; his customers dropped away; his business began to decline, and his creditors to question his financial soundness. There was a general slump in his affairs, and he finally "went to pieces."

We can conquer our moods; we can think correctly; we can be what we will to be; we can work miracles with ourselves by the power of affirmative or creative thought; we can make ourselves magnets to attract the conditions we desire, instead of repellent forces.

"Man is so made," says Pascal, "that by dint of telling him he is a fool, he believes it; and by dint of telling himself so, he makes himself believe it." The converse is also true. Many people, by dwelling on their faults, only aggravate them. By constantly picturing them in the mind they help to fasten them more firmly. It is impossible for us to become what we wish to be while we hold the opposite thought. The only way to overcome evil conditions and to upbuild is to think constantly happy, helpful, loving, optimistic thoughts.

When a doctor is called to prescribe for any one who has swallowed poison, he immediately administers an antidote. So, when we are suffering from wrong thinking, it is because we have been poisoned by vicious thoughts, and the only way in which we can get relief or cure ourselves is by taking an antidote in the shape of right thinking. If a lamp should explode and the oil catch fire, we would not think of trying to put out the flames by pouring on more oil. We would, instead, pour on some chemical extinguisher which would immediately put out the fire. When one is aflame with passion, or afire with hatred, jealousy, or revengeful feelings, the flames will not be put out by adding more anger, more hatred, or more jealousy. A love-thought is the natural antidote to all angry, vengeful, or uncharitable emotions.

If you are morose, moody, or despondent; if you have a habit of worrying or fretting about things, or any other fault which hinders your growth or progress, think persistently of the opposite virtue and practise it until it is yours by force of habit.

When you feel unhappy and out of sorts with all the world nothing is more certain than that nursing such feelings aggravates them. Hold just the opposite thought from that which depresses you and you will naturally reverse the mood. The imagination has great power to change an unpleasant thought or experience. When you are the victim of vicious moods just say to yourself, "This is all unreal; it has nothing to do with my higher and better self, for the Creator never intended me to be dominated by such dark pictures." Persistently recall the most delightful experiences, the happiest days of your life. Look on some beautiful object in art or in nature, or read a passage in some helpful, uplifting book. Hold persistently in the mind such things as you have enjoyed; drive out the failure-thoughts by thinking of the successful things you have accomplished. Call hope to your aid, and picture a bright, successful future. Surround yourself with happy thoughts for a few minutes and you will be surprised to see how all the ghosts of blackness and gloom, — all thoughts which have worried and haunted you — have gone out of sight. They cannot bear the light. Light, joy, gladness, and harmony are your best protectors; discord, darkness, and sickness cannot exist where they are.

One of the brightest and most cheerful women I ever knew told me that she was prone to fits of depression or "blues," but that she learned to conquer them by forcing herself to sing a bright, joyous song, or to play a lively air on the piano whenever she felt an "attack" coming on.

Everything which depresses or arouses violent passions is a waster of mental force. Every time a wrong thought is indulged there is a waste of mental energy, of achievement-power. All wrong thinking is negative, and the mind can only create when it is positive and affirmative.

Until we can control our moods and marshal our thoughts at will, as a general marshals his army, we can never do our best work. We must master our thoughts. or be their slave. No man who is at the mercy of his moods is a free man. He only is free who can rise to his dominion in spite of his mental enemies. If a man must consult his moods every morning to see whether he can do his best work or not during the day; if he must look at his mental thermometer when he rises to see whether his courage is rising or falling; if he says to himself, "I can do a good day's work to-day if the 'blues' don't strike me, if some unfortunate phase of business does not come up and disturb my equilibrium, or if I can only manage to keep my temper," he is a slave; he cannot be successful or happy.

How different is the outlook of a man who feels confident every morning that he is going to do a man's work, the very best that he is capable of, during the day. How superbly he carries himself who knows that he can work out the Creator's design each day, and has no fear, or doubt, or anxiety as to what he can accomplish. He feels that he is master of himself, and knows to a certainty that no moods or conditions have power to hinder him. He has come into his dominion.

Amid the feverish rush and turmoil of modern life, the fierce competition, and the nerve-exhausting struggle for existence in which the majority are engaged, we see here and there serene souls who impress us with a sense of power and of calm, unhesitating assurance, and who travel toward their goal with the rhythmic majesty of the stars. They have learned how to think correctly; they have mastered the secret of successful living.

It is true this supreme self-control, which enables a man to rise to his highest power, is one of the ultimate lessons of culture; but it is the first step to great achievement and is possible to all.

Sometime we shall all learn better than to harbor, even for an instant, any suicidal thought or emotion. We shall no more dream of entertaining thoughts of fear, envy, or jealousy, or worrying, fretful, or anxious thoughts, than we would of entertaining thieves or murderers in our homes. The time will come when intelligent people will no more indulge in fits of anger, will no more indulge in uncharitable thoughts, feelings of hatred or ill-will, or gloomy, depressing, downward-tending thoughts, than they would take poison into the system.

Thousands of people who never amount to much could do the work of giants if they could only conquer their moods.

XXV.

LET YOUR DECISION BE FINAL.

THE day before the terrible disaster at St. Pierre, the Italian bark, "Orsalina," was taking her cargo aboard, but her skipper, Captain Marino Leboffe, became so alarmed by the threatening appearance of the volcano that he decided to stop loading and sail away at once. The shippers for whom he was acting protested, and threatened to have him arrested if he should attempt to leave the harbor with only half his cargo aboard. But the captain was immovable. To their angry remonstrances and repeated assurance that Mt. Pelée was not dangerous, his firm reply was, "I don't know anything about Mt. Pelée, but if Vesuvius should look as your volcano does this morning I would get out of Naples and I am going to get out of here. I would rather sail with half a cargo than run such a risk as a man would run here."

Twenty-four hours later, the shippers and the two custom-house officers who had tried to arrest Captain Leboffe were dead at St. Pierre, while the "Orsalina," with her captain and crew, was safe on the high seas, heading toward France. A strong will and an unalterable decision had won, where weakness and yielding vacillation would have led to destruction.

IN THE CHEERING-UP BUSINESS.

The great demand of to-day is for the strong, vigorous, positive man, the man who not only makes up his mind, but does so with firmness, and, when he has considered all the circumstances and conditions of the matter he is called upon to decide, does so once for all, and then throws it off his mind and passes to something else. Such a man has usually superior executive ability. He cannot only make a programme, but he can also carry it out. He cannot only decide upon a course, but he can also execute it to a finish.

Every watch has an unseen spring back of the dial which compels the wheels to revolve and makes the hands mark the time with precision; so, beneath the works of every great enterprise, at the head of every great establishment, although not often seen by the public, is a strong character of this kind, a man with an iron grip, who makes things go and forces the wheels of the machine around, regulating their motion with precision. There is no going back of him; his decision is absolute, definite, final. Others can consider, advise, or suggest, but he is the man who makes the programme and sees that it is carried out. He is the dominating power. Everything else must point to him, and all others must get their cues or orders from him. If he steps out or ceases to act, the institution is like a watch with a broken mainspring. The wheels are all there, and everything else is in place, but the power is gone and nothing moves. The iron hand, the decisive power back of it all, has failed to lend its impulse. The splendid business which A. T. Stewart had built up went to pieces when the great executive and organizing force that had guided it was removed. The famous old "New York Ledger," which Robert Bonner, by his audacious and original business methods, had raised from an insignificant little financial sheet known as the "Merchant's Ledger" to be the leading story paper of this country, began to decline immediately after the master-mind which had made it ceased to be its inspiration.

There is only one of these great leaders to thousands of followers. It is easy to trail, to lean, or to hang onto the one who leads, but it takes courage, grit, and stamina to be original, prompt, and decisive, to stand squarely on one's own feet, and to trust entirely to one's own judgment.

If you are a vacillator, if you have acquired a habit of hesitating, or of weighing and considering and reconsidering, never quite knowing what you want, you will never be a leader. This is not the stuff of which leaders are made; for, whatever else a leader may lack, he knows his own mind. He knows what he wants, and makes straight for it. He may make mistakes; he may fall down now and then, but he gets up promptly and always pushes on.

The man who decides quickly can afford to make mistakes; for no matter how many he makes he will get on faster than he who is timid, vacillating and so afraid of taking a wrong course that he dares not start out to do anything. Those who wait for certainties, or stand on the brink of the stream waiting for somebody to push them in, never reach the other shore.

One of the most pitiable objects in the world is the man who is forever hanging trembling in the balance, who never knows which way to turn, who is the prey of conflicting opinions and the victim of the greatest pressure, who follows the counsel of the last man who advises him, who moves along the line of least resistance, and who does not feel within himself the power to decide things. The very reputation of being cursed with a yielding disposition, of being easily moved from your conviction, or of being unstable in your opinions is fatal to all confidence, — to credit.

A great many people seem to have a mortal dread of deciding things. They don't dare to take the responsibility, because they don't know what it may lead to. They are afraid that if they should decide upon one thing to-day, something better may come up to-morrow and cause them to regret their first decision. These habitual waverers so completely lose their self-confidence that they do not dare to trust themselves to decide anything of importance. Many of them ruin naturally fine minds by nursing the fatal habit of indecision.

I know a man who never closes anything of any importance if he can possibly avoid it. Everything is left open for further evidence. He will not seal his letters until the very last minute lest he may want to change something. Time and again I have seen him tear open the seal of an envelope, after it was stamped and ready to mail, in order to make some change. He has even been known to telegraph to people to return his letters without opening them. Although this man is a great worker, a man of fine character, and splendid friend, he has such a reputation of being whimsical and uncertain in his judgment, always ready to reconsider anything that he has in hand, or to go over what he has already done, that he has never won the confidence of business men with hard sense. Everybody who knows him feels sorry for his weakness, but does not want to trust him with anything of importance.

Another victim of vacillation whom I know is a lady whose character in other respects is admirable. Whenever she wishes to buy anything she makes a tour of all the stores in her city where the articles she wants are sold. She drifts from counter to counter, from department to department, from store to store, pulling over the goods on the counters, holding them up, and looking at them from different standpoints, but never knowing exactly what she wants. She would like to look at something "a little different" in shade, or at "a little different" style of goods. She cannot quite tell what will be most becoming to her. She will try on all the hats in the shopping district, look at all the dresses, and tire out all the clerks by her questions, but will probably go home without buying anything. If she does purchase, she is in doubt as to whether or not she has done just the right thing, wonders if she would better take it back and change it, and asks the opinion of everybody she knows. She wants something that is warm, and yet not too heavy or too warm. She wants something that will be comfortable on both a hot day and a cold one; something that will be appropriate for the mountains or the seashore, for the church or the opera, — some combination impossible to procure. She seldom buys anything without changing it two or three times, yet is never satisfied.

Such wavering and inconstancy of mind are fatal to all character building. No one who is thus cursed will ever have any close-knit fibre of character or stamina timber. Such things ruin one's confidence in himself and his own judgment, and are destructive to all mental effectiveness.

Your judgment must dwell in the depths of your

nature, like the calm waters in the depths of the sea, out of the reach of the waves of emotion, passion, or moods, or the advice or criticism of others, and beyond the reach of superficial disturbance. This is the kind of judgment that is always sought in any matter of weight or importance, — one which is beyond the reach of the influence of anything but the right. One of the tragedies of life is to see magnificent ability held down by some little weakness, when, perhaps, most of the faculties are strong and vigorous. Thousands of people, to-day, are struggling along in mediocrity with ability enough to have taken them to the heights where excellence dwells, but for one lack in their nature, — ability to decide quickly and finally. The tragedies of untrusted judgments have given the world more failures than actual incompetence.

An engineer who starts to build a bridge and then keeps finding better places to put his piers, and wondering whether he has selected the best location or not, will never get the bridge across the river. He must decide, then go ahead and build the bridge, no matter what obstacles he may strike. So it is with the builder of character, he must decide finally what he will do, and then make for his goal, refusing to look back or be moved from his course.

Tens of thousands of young people with good health, good education, and good ability are standing on the end of a bridge at life's crossing. They hope they are on the right way, they think they are doing the right thing, and yet they do not dare to burn the bridge they have just crossed. They want a chance for retreat in case they have made a mistake. They cannot bear the thought of cutting off all possibility of turning back.

They lack the power to decide conclusively what course they will take.

These young people are in danger of wrecking their lives by their hesitation. If they would only make up their minds to burn their bridges behind them, and thus concentrate their powers on one definite point, they would immeasurably strengthen their chances of success. All of their resources would then rush to their assistance, buttress them against obstacles, and make their victory certain. But while there is a doubt in their minds, and they hold the path of retreat open, they will never amount to much.

If indecision runs in the blood you inherit, arouse yourself and strangle this insidious foe to your achievement before it saps your energy and ruins your life chance. Do not wait until to-morrow, but begin to-day. Compel yourself to develop the opposite quality by the constant practice of firm decision. No matter how simple the thing you are called upon to decide, be it the choice of a hat or the color or style of a garment, do not vacillate. Throw all the light possible on whatever you have in hand for decision; weigh and consider it from every point of view; call your common sense and best judgment to your aid before reaching a conclusion, and then, when you have once made your decision, let it be final. Let there be no going back, no reconsidering, and no opening the matter up for further discussion. Be firm and positive. Declare the polls closed.

Persist in this course until the habit of firm decision becomes fixed and you will be surprised to see what it will do for you, both in increasing your confidence in yourself and that of others in you. You may make mistakes in the beginning, but the strength and reliance you will gain in your own judgment will more than compensate for these. The power to decide firmly strikes at the very marrow of ability. If you cannot do this your life ship will always be adrift; you will never be anchored. You will drift about on the seas at the mercy of storms and tempests, and will never make your port.

XXVI.

GREAT DETERMINATION AND LITTLE TALENT.

How can we account for the fact that many of the greatest things in the world are done by one-talent men, while the ten-talent, the versatile man is never heard from? Everywhere we see young men succeeding apparently out of all proportion to their ability, and we do not understand it at all. We cannot understand why the boy who was at the foot of our class in school or college has distanced us in the great life race, for he did not have half the ability we possessed. We laughed at him at school, but, somehow, he has focused his energies upon one thing and, like a tortoise, he kept plodding until he "arrived." He has managed to keep ahead, to accumulate a competence with one talent, while our ten talents are still drifting without aim or results.

The very consciousness of being dull and stupid has spurred many a boy on to make the most of what little ability he had. The very humiliation of being told so often by teachers and parents that he is not bright makes him determined that he will not be a nobody. The very comparison of himself with his brilliant brother has perhaps made him set his teeth with a resolution to show that the brother has not absorbed all the ability of the family.

Discovering or having it impressed upon him how limited his abilities are, he makes great efforts, and not being versatile, he does not have the temptation to dissipate his energies on a score of things, but simply develops his one talent and makes the most of it. He can concentrate and focus his powers more easily than can the ten-talent man. He does not have to meet constantly the arguments on this hand and on that, that perhaps he could do something else better. He knows if he succeeds at all it must be by developing his one talent, and he focuses all his attention upon it.

We hear a great deal of talk about genius, talent, luck, chance, cleverness, and fine manners playing a large part in one's success. Leaving out luck and chance, we grant that all these elements are important factors in the battle of life. Yet the possession of any or all of them, unaccompanied by a definite aim, a determined purpose, will not insure success. Whatever else may have been lacking in the giants of the race, the men who have been conspicuously successful, we shall find that they all had one characteristic in common — doggedness and persistence of purpose.

It does not matter how clever a youth may be, whether he leads his class in college or outshines all the other boys in his community, he will never succeed if he lacks this essential of determined persistence. Many men who might have made brilliant musicians, artists, teachers, lawyers, able physicians or surgeons, in spite of predictions to the contrary, have fallen short of success because they were deficient in this quality.

Persistency of purpose is a power. It creates confidence in others. Everybody believes in the determined

ULYSSES S. GRANT.

man. When he undertakes anything his battle is half won, because not only he himself, but every one who knows him, believes that he will accomplish whatever he sets out to do. People know that it is useless to oppose a man who uses his stumbling-blocks as stepping-stones; who is not afraid of defeat; who never, in spite of calumny or criticism, shrinks from his task; who never shirks responsibility; who always keeps his compass pointed to the north star of his purpose, no matter what storms may rage about him.

What good would it do to oppose such a man as Grant? One might as well attempt to snub the sun. There were many more brilliant men in the Northern army, but no other was so dogged, so persistent in purpose as Grant. He could see but one thing — the triumphant end. It did not matter how long it might take to reach that end. It must be fought out on that line "if it took all summer."

Napoleon was much more brilliant than Wellington, but was not a match for him in dogged persistence. The iron duke could stick to a losing campaign with as much determination as to a winning one. He did n't know how to beat a retreat.

The persistent man never stops to consider whether he is succeeding or not. The only question with him is how to push ahead, to get a little further along, a little nearer his goal. Whether it lead over mountains, rivers or morasses, he must reach it. Every other consideration is sacrificed to this one dominant purpose.

The success of a dull or average youth and the failure of a brilliant one is a constant surprise in American history. But if the different cases are closely analyzed we shall find that the explanation lies in the staying power of the seemingly dull boy, the ability to stand firm as a rock under all circumstances, to allow nothing to divert him from his purpose, while the brilliant but erratic boy, lacking the rudder of a firm purpose, neutralizes his power and wastes his energy by dissipating them in several directions.

We often find that boys who have educated themselves in the country, almost without schooling or teachers, make the most vigorous thinkers. They may not be quite as polished or cultivated in some ways, but they have something better than polish, and that is mental vigor, originality of method, and independence. They do not lean upon their schooling, or depend upon their diplomas; necessity has been their teacher, and they have been forced to act for themselves and be practical; they know little of theories, but they know what will work. They have gained power by solving their own problems. Such self-educated, self-made men carry weight in their communities because they are men of power and think vigorously and strongly; they have learned to concentrate the mind.

Self-help is the only help that will make strong, vigorous lives. Self-reliance is a great educator and early poverty a good teacher. Necessity has ever been the priceless spur which has called man out of himself and spurred him on to his goal.

Grit is more than a match for almost any handicap. It overcomes obstacles and abolishes difficulties. It is the man who makes an opportunity and does not wait for it — the man who helps himself and does not wait to be helped — that makes the strong thinker and vigorous operator.

It is he who dares to be himself and to work by his own programme, without imitating others, who wins.

If you will greatly succeed in life, it is of the first importance that your individuality, your independence, your originality, be so trained that you will not be lost in the crowd. No one else can solve your problem, or work out your riddle. You stand or fall by it. Your happiness, your well-being, your success and your destiny hang upon your carrying out the programme the Creator has given you.

No matter how skilfully constructed or how powerful the locomotive may be, unless the water used to run it is boiling, the train will not move an inch. What the boiling water is to a locomotive, enthusiasm is to a man. No matter how great his ability or diversified his talents, unless he is filled with that enthusiasm which generates energy, great motive power, as the boiling water generates the steam which propels the train, he will never accomplish anything noteworthy. Every successful person, whatever his profession or occupation, is filled with this stimulating force. It is this which enables him to overleap obstacles, to spurn hardship and privation to dare any danger in order to reach his goal.

This immortal fire kindles sleeping powers, stimulates latent energies, and arouses resources undreamed of before. It multiplies ability and often takes the place of talent.

XXVII.

MINIMIZING DIFFICULTIES.

THE world has little use for the weak-kneed, the faint-hearted, but the conqueror who carries victory in his very presence, who overcomes opposition which appalls weak minds, who does not skip his difficult problems, who conquers everything which gets in his way, is always in demand. People who accomplish but little usually have a genius for seeing difficulties in the way of everything they undertake. Their imaginations conjure up obstacles which rise in their pathway, like giants or great mountain peaks, and paralyze their courage. They can see them a long way off. They begin to look for them as soon as they plan any course of action; they wait for them, and, of course, they find them.

These people seem to wear obstacle glasses and they see nothing but difficulties. There is always an "if" or a "but" or a "can't" in the way, — just enough to keep them from taking the necessary step or making energetic effort to get what they want.

They do not think there is any use trying to get a situation which they see advertised because there will probably be a hundred other applicants ahead of them when they get there. They see so many people out of employment that they have no hope of getting a position for themselves; or, if they have one, they see so many obstacles to their advancement, so many ahead of them, so many favored by their employer, that when there is a vacancy they stand no show for promotion.

No man can rise to anything very great who allows himself to be tripped or thwarted by impediments. His achievement will be in proportion to his ability to rise triumphantly over the stumbling-blocks which trip others.

When I hear a young man whining that he has no chance, complaining that fate has doomed him to mediocrity, that he can never get a start for himself, but must always work for somebody else; when I see him finding unconquerable obstacles everywhere, when he tells me that he could do this or that if he could only get a start, if somebody would help him, I know there is very poor success material in him, — that he is not made of the stuff that rises. He acknowledges that he is not equal to the emergencies which confront him. He confesses his weakness, his inability to cope with obstacles which others surmount. When a man tells us that luck is against him, that he cannot see any way of doing what he would like to do, he admits that he is not master of the situation, that he must give way to opposition because he is not big enough or strong enough to surmount it. He probably has n't lime enough in his backbone to hold a straw erect.

There is a weakness in the man who always sees a lion in the way of what he wants to do, whose determination is not strong enough to overcome the obstacle. He has not the inclination to buckle down to solid, hard work. He wants success, but he does not want it badly enough to pay the price. The desire to drift along, to take things easy, to have a good time, overbalances ambition.

Obstacles will look large or small to you according to whether you are large or small.

People who have a tendency to magnify difficulties lack the stamina and grit necessary to win. They are not willing to sacrifice a little comfort and pleasure. They see so much hardship in working their own way through college or starting in business without capital that they do neither. These people always look for somebody to help them, to give them a boost.

When a boy tells me that he just yearns for an education, that he longs to go to college, but that he has no one to help him as other boys have, that, if he had a rich father to send him to college, he could make something of himself, I know perfectly well that that boy does not yearn for an education, but that he would simply like to have it if it could be gotten without much effort. He does not long for it as Lincoln did. When a boy to-day says that he cannot go to college, — although deaf, dumb, and blind girls manage to do it, — I know that he has such a knack of seeing difficulties that he will not only miss college, but will probably also miss most of what is worth while in life.

The young man who, after making up his mind what he wants to do in the world, begins to hunt up obstacles in his path, to magnify them, to brood over them until they become mountains, and then to wait for new ones to develop, is not a man to take hold of great enterprises. The man who stops to weigh and consider every possible danger or objection never amounts to anything. He is a small man, made for little things. He walks around an obstacle, and goes as far as he can easily, but when the going gets hard he stops.

The strong man, the positive, decisive soul who has a programme, and who is determined to carry it out, cuts his way to his goal regardless of difficulties. It is the weak-kneed man, the discouraged man, who turns aside, who takes a crooked path to his goal. Men who achieve things, who get things done, do not spend time haggling over perplexities, or wondering whether they can overcome them. A penny held close to the eye will shut out the sun. When a man lies down on the ground to see what is ahead of him, a rock may hide a mountain. A small man holds petty difficulties so closely in view that great objects beyond are entirely shut out of sight. Great minds keep their eyes on the goal. They hold the end so persistently in view, and it looks so grand and desirable, that the intermediate steps, no matter how perplexing, are of comparatively little importance. The great man asks but one question, "Can the thing be done?" not "How many difficulties will I run across?" If it is within the reach of possibility, all hindrances must be pushed aside.

We meet these trouble-borrowing, difficulty-seeing people everywhere. There is usually one or more on every school board and church board, every board of directors or trustees, who always sees difficulties which do not appear to the others, and if everything depended upon these people nothing would ever be accomplished. Nearly every invention, discovery, or achievement which has blest the world would have failed had the calamity-howlers, the objection-seers been listened to.

The youth who is bound to win may see difficulties,

but he is not afraid of them because he feels that they are no match for his grit. He feels within himself a power infinitely superior. He knows perfectly well that undaunted pluck can annihilate them. To his determination they do not exist. The Alps did not exist to Napoleon, not because they were not formidable mountains, almost impassable in midwinter, but because he felt that he was greater than they. His generals could see the Alps, with all their terrors, and thought they were impassable; but the mighty general saw only victory on the green plains beyond the eternal snow.

You will find that the habit of minimizing annoyances or difficulties, of making the best of everything that comes to you, of magnifying the pleasant and the agreeable and reducing to the least possible importance everything that is disagreeable or unpleasant, will help you wonderfully not only in your work but also in your attainment of happiness. It transforms the disagreeable into the agreeable, takes the drudgery out of distasteful tasks, eases the jolts of life wonderfully, and it is worth infinitely more than money. You will find yourself growing to be a larger, completer man. The sunny, buoyant, cheerful soul manages, without losing his equilibrium, to glide over difficulties and annoyances which throw others off their balance and make them miserable and disagreeable.

The Creator never put the grandest of his creations — man — at the mercy of petty trifles, or intended him to be crushed by obstacles. Character was never intended to be ruined by irritation. But even the Creator cannot make a man who is determined to use blue glasses see things in a white light. It all depends upon the color of the glasses you adopt, — your own mental attitude.

MINIMIZING DIFFICULTIES.

Every man has within him the power of changing the blue into white, the disagreeable into the agreeable; every one has the crystal lens which may resolve even murky light into rainbow hues.

No man ever amounted to much in the world until he learned to put out of the way things which would trip him, or to get rid, at any cost, of the things which block his passage. Self is the greatest stumbling-block. Our own selfishness, our desire for comfort, for pleasure, is the greatest obstacle in the path of all progress. Timidity, doubt, and fear are great enemies. Guard your weak point, conquer yourself, and you can conquer everything else.

It makes great difference how you approach a difficulty. Obstacles are like wild animals. They are cowards but they will bluff you if they can. If they see you are afraid of them, if you stand and hesitate, if you take your eyes from theirs, they are liable to spring upon you; but if you do not flinch, if you look them squarely in the eye, they will slink out of sight. So difficulties flee before absolute fearlessness, though they are very real and formidable to the timid and hesitating, and grow larger and larger and more formidable with vacillating contemplation.

Charlotte Perkins Gilman, in her little poem, "An Obstacle," describes a traveler struggling up a mountain side, bent on important business, and bearing a heavy load, when suddenly a huge obstacle spread itself across his path. He was dismayed. He politely begged the obstacle to get out of his path. It did not move. He became angry and abused it. He knelt down and prayed it to let him pass. It remained immovable. Then the traveler sat down helpless before it, when a sudden inspiration seized him. Let him tell in his own words how he settled the matter:

> "I took my hat, I took my stick,
> My load I settled fair,
> I approached that awful incubus
> With an absent-minded air —
> And I walked directly through him
> As if he was n't there!"

Most of our obstacles would melt away if, instead of cowering before them, we should make up our minds to walk boldly through them.

XXVIII.

FORTUNE SEED.

IF a person who has received a comfortable salary for five or ten years suddenly finds himself out of a position, without any money saved up, he is quite likely to blame his luck, instead of looking at the matter with a dispassionate mind and realizing that experience is putting before him, in the most convincing manner, a lesson which he needs to learn by heart.

If, instead of bemoaning his "luck," he will listen, a still, small voice will whisper to him of nickels, dimes, and even dollars foolishly squandered; nickels, dimes, and dollars spent which have not yielded their value in enjoyment. Money spent on legitimate pleasures need never be regretted. Legitimate pleasures are those which do not leave a bad taste in the mouth, but, instead, bestow delightful memories that no amount of hardship can deprive one of.

The writer knows of a person whose income has unexpectedly been cut off, leaving him quite unprepared. For years he has lived up to the limit of his salary giving no thought to the future. "Think of it," he remarked, desperately, "had I but saved only ten cents a day for the last fifteen years, and I could have done so without ever missing it, I should now have five hundred and forty-seven dollars and fifty cents, not allowing for accrued interest. But I might have saved a great deal more than that, without foregoing any real pleasures. 'T is maddening to think of such folly, and I deserve the hard time I am having."

But, perhaps, you think that the family of a laboring man could not save ten cents a day without a great deal of self-sacrifice. It is certainly no over-statement of fact to assume that the average workingman in this country might save five cents a day without undergoing deprivations. The amount is too small to be worth while. Let us see?

Suppose that a young man of twenty-one should make a vow to put away at least five cents a day, each day in the year, and not to touch his savings for ten years. Do you realize that, at the end of that time, he would have one hundred and eighty-two dollars and fifty cents to his credit, as a result of putting away an amount so small that he would never miss it? Many enormous fortunes have grown from a smaller capital than this.

If a man has good brains, energy, and, at the age of thirty-one, a capital of one hundred and eighty-two dollars and fifty cents, there is no reason why, at the age of forty-one, he should not have a very snug nest-egg indeed, if he be a man of ordinary ability.

If, on the other hand, he has the money-making talent, there is no reason why he should not be well started on the road to wealth. If in ten years, his earliest and best years, he can accumulate but five cents a day, he will never become very rich.

The power of small things is one of the most important facts of life and too much stress cannot be laid upon it. It is absurd and illogical to despise the units when there can be no tens and hundreds without them. A

SIR THOMAS LIPTON.

man alone may be puny and insignificant; but, multiplied, he constitutes the power which dominates the earth.

One penny may seem to you a very insignificant thing, but it is the small seed from which fortunes spring. If we want to raise a flower or vegetable, we procure the seed, plant it in good soil, and do all that we can to facilitate its growth; or we may be fortunate enough to procure a half-grown plant; but sometime, somewhere, somebody planted the seed.

The penny is nothing in the world but the seed of that wonderful growth which the best of us cannot help admiring, and for which all of us long — the fortune plant! If you would have one of these wonderful plants for your own, if you dream of sitting at ease under its branches in your old age, go about it in a rational way. From this moment, treat that little disk of copper, with the head of an Indian on one side and "ONE CENT" on the other, with the respect that a fortune seed deserves. Don't scatter and waste seeds so valuable, but plant them in the soil which will foster them — the savings bank.

There is hardly an able-bodied laborer who might not become financially independent if he would but carefully husband his receipts and guard against the little leaks of needless expense. But, unfortunately, this is the one thing which the working-man finds it the hardest to do. There are a hundred laborers who are willing to work hard to every half-dozen who are willing properly to husband their earnings. Instead of hoarding a small percentage of their receipts, so as to provide against sickness or want of employment, they eat and drink up their earnings as they go, and thus, in the first financial crash, when mills and factories "shut down" and capitalists lock up their cash instead of using it in great enterprises, they are ruined. Men who thus live "from hand to mouth," never keeping more than a day's march ahead of actual want, are little better off than slaves.

"I have often been asked to define the true secret of success," says Sir Thomas Lipton. "It is thrift in all its phases and, principally, thrift as applied to saving. A young man may have many friends, but he will find none so steadfast, so constant, so ready to respond to his wants, so capable of pushing him ahead, as a little leather-covered book, with the name of a bank on its cover. Saving is the first great principle of success. It creates independence, it gives a young man standing, it fills him with vigor, it stimulates him with proper energy; in fact, it brings to him the best part of any success, — happiness and contentment. If it were possible to inject the quality of saving into every boy we would have a great many more real men."

"Provided he has some ability and good sense to start with," said Philip D. Armour, "there is no reason why any young man who is thrifty, honest, and economical should not accumulate money and attain so-called success in life." When asked to what qualities he attributed his own success, Mr. Armour said: "I think that thrift and economy had much to do with it. I owe much to my mother's training and to a good line of Scotch ancestors who have always been thrifty and economical."

"Every boy should realize, in starting out, that he can never accumulate money unless he acquires the habit of saving," says Russell Sage. "Even if he can save only a few cents at the beginning, it is better than saving nothing at all; and he will find, as the months go on, that it becomes easier for him to lay by a part of his earnings. It is surprising how fast an account in a savings bank can be made to grow, and the boy who starts one and keeps it up stands a good chance of spending a prosperous old age. Some people who spend every cent of their income on their living expenses are always bewailing the fact that they have never become rich."

" The first thing that a man should learn to do," says Andrew Carnegie, " is to save his money. By saving his money he promotes thrift, — the most valued of all habits. Thrift is the great fortune-maker. It draws the line between the savage and the civilized man. Thrift not only develops the fortune, but it develops, also, the man's character."

XXIX.

ENTANGLING ALLIANCES.

Recently a young woman in New York became fascinated by a young man whom she met accidentally, and, after only a few days' acquaintance, was married to him. She did not look up his history and did not know anything about his past. While on their wedding trip the bridegroom was arrested for theft, and it was found that he had been in jail several times before. The bride was heart-broken, but she could not retrieve the false step that linked her fate with that of a convicted thief. By not taking a little precaution this innocent girl has practically ruined her life.

It is the easiest thing in the world to slide into the meshes of entanglements which will cripple our advance or mar our reputations. How many careless young girls are led unconsciously into alliances with young men of whom they know practically nothing and wake up to find themselves entangled for life!

How many men in our large cities, rich, and, apparently, possessing everything to make them happy, are being blackmailed to-day, their lives made a hell on earth by the partners of their entangling alliances. How many homes are wrecked every year, and how many innocent and unsuspecting children made to blush with

Always your friend
Andrew Carnegie

tims of entanglements of all kinds in this country to-day who, if they could only gain the ears of the young just starting out in life, would repeat to them Washington's words of warning.

Is there a sadder picture than that of a promising young man of great ability, conscious of power which he has no opportunity to use to advantage, and mocked by an ambition which he cannot satisfy, because he is hopelessly in debt or so bound by other self-forged chains that he cannot extricate himself? Instead of being a king and dominating his environment, he is a slave to his entanglement, or is dogged for years by creditors.

Keep yourself free. Keep clear from complications of all kinds that may possibly compromise your manhood, your womanhood. An entanglement, whatever its nature, is imprisonment, no less terrible because it is voluntary. If your brain is intact, your mind unburdened, your hands and all your faculties free, you can do great things even with small money capital, or, perhaps, even without any. But when you are ground under the heel of debt and are not at liberty to act of your own accord, but are pushed hither and thither by those to whom you are under obligations or with whom you have formed entangling alliances, you cannot accomplish much. You are a bondman, not a free man.

There are hundreds of men to-day, in middle life or older, working in ordinary positions who are as able as or abler than the men who employ them, but who were so anxious to "get rich quick" that they fell an easy prey to smooth, long-headed promoters. They got so entangled in wildcat schemes and plausible speculations that they have never been able to free themselves. Good, honest men and women in this country are struggling with superhuman efforts under loads which almost crush them, and are barely getting a living, who could do wonders if they were only free. But every avenue of opportunity seems closed to them because they are not in a position to seize whatever chance may offer, — are not free to work it out. Everything they do is done at great disadvantage. They have to employ personal work and sheer force to accomplish what a little planning would do if they had not lost their money in some foolish investment, or were not so tied up by mortgages and debts that they are practically business prisoners. They cannot go where they would, but where they must. They are pushed instead of pushing; forced instead of forcing. They do not choose; iron circumstances compel them.

I know one of these victims who earns five hundred dollars a month, but for years half of his salary has gone for what business men call "paying for a dead horse." When quite a young man he made a foolish investment, in which he not only lost every dollar he laid up, but also gave notes for a large amount, which fall due every three months. He cannot get free from these notes without going into bankruptcy, which he is too honorable to do, and so his whole life has been handicapped. He is now fifty years old, with several sons and daughters, whom he has not been able to educate as he was ambitious to do. The comfort and happiness of his family, as well as his own peace of mind, have been ruined by this ghost-debt which will not down. He has lived all these years in constant fear that he might be sick, or that something might happen to him, and that his wife and children might suffer in consequence.

The result of all this is not only a disappointed ambition, but the man has also lost his hopeful disposition, his buoyancy, and natural optimism, and has become sour and pessimistic. His monotonous life of compulsory service, of slavery to a foolish transaction, entered into without investigation, way back in his young manhood, has crushed all the spirit out of him. He has practically given up the thought of ever doing anything more than make a bare living for himself and his family. Existence has become a mere joyless drudgery because in a weak moment he mortgaged his whole future.

What freedom or power has a man for a creative, productive career under such conditions as these? Shut up in the prison of debt, bound hand and foot by entanglements from which, perhaps, he can never get release, how can he work out his life plan? How can he realize his aspirations?

Struggling just for something to eat and something to wear, while forced to give up most of one's earnings for past errors, is not life. It is not freedom. It is slavery. It is slow strangulation.

The mania for getting rich — the mad, false idea that we must have money — has played worse havoc among ambitious people than war or pestilence. A member of the Chicago Board of Trade says that the men and women of this country contribute a hundred million dollars a year to the sharpers who promise to make them rich quick. They work the same old scheme of a confidential letter and shrewd baiting, until the victim parts with his money. Thousands are plodding along in poverty and deprivation, chagrined and humiliated because they have not been able to get up in the world or to realize their ambitions, for the reason that they succumbed to the scheme of some smooth promoter, who hypnotized them into the belief that they could make a great deal very quickly out of a very little.

The great fever of trying to make one dollar earn five dollars is growing more and more contagious. We see even women secretly going into brokers' offices and "bucket shops," investing everything they have in all sorts of schemes, drawing their deposits out of the banks, sometimes pawning their jewelry, — even their engagement rings, — and borrowing, hoping to make a lot of money before their husbands or families find it out and then to surprise them with the results; but in most cases what they invest is hopelessly lost.

Thousands of young Americans are so tied up by financial or other entanglements, even before they get fairly started in their life-work, that they can only transmute a tithe of their real ability or their splendid energies into that which will count in their lives. A large part of it is lost on the way up, as the energy of the coal is nearly all lost before it reaches the electric bulb.

Don't tie yourself or your money up. Don't risk all your savings in any scheme, no matter how much it may promise. Don't invest your hard-earned money in anything without first making a thorough and searching investigation. Do not be misled by those who tell you that it is "now or never," and that, if you wait, you are liable to lose the best thing that ever came to you. Make up your mind that if you lose your money you will not lose your head, and that you will not invest in anything until you thoroughly understand all about it. There are plenty of good things waiting. If you miss one, there are hundreds of others. People will tell you that the opportunity will go by and you will lose a great chance to make money if you do not act promptly. But take your time, and investigate. Make it a cast-iron rule never to invest in any enterprise until you have gone to the very bottom of it, and, if it is not so sound that level-headed men will put money in it, do not touch it. The habit of investigating before you embark in any business will be a happiness-protector, a fortune-protector, and an ambition-protector as well.

Young people often get involved with questionable characters, and, before they are aware of it, their reputations become smirched. They do not choose their friends with discretion, or they compromise themselves socially, politically, or in a business way, innocently, perhaps, but with the same result. Before they realize how it has happened, either their characters have received a stain which will not wash out, or they find themselves in an unfortunate, embarrassing position.

Look out for your record, young man and young woman. Keep it clean and yourself unentangled. As you value freedom, the boon of a clean reputation, and an unobstructed passage in your upward climb, do not tie yourself up, — financially, socially, morally, or in any other way. Keep yourself clear of crippling obligations of all kinds, so that you can act with freedom and with untrammeled faculties. Keep your manhood, your womanhood, and independence so that you can always look the world squarely in the face. Do not put yourself in a position where you must apologize or cringe or bow your head or crawl before anybody.

A little ability with freedom and a persistent determination is better than genius so tied up that it cannot act. A productive, effective mind must be untrammeled. What is the use of having a giant's intellect if you bind your faculties in such a way that you must do a pygmy's work, the work of mediocrity ? Keep your freedom at all costs.

XXX.

BUSINESS INTEGRITY.

"WILL you be honest, if I buy you?" asked a would-be buyer of a young negro, in the old days of human traffic. "I will be honest, whether you buy me or not," replied the slave.

We hear much about honesty as the best policy. It is recommended even by those who say that they have tried both ways, and ought to know. Yet to be honest anyway, whatever comes of it, is the first thought of every one who carried his manhood into his business.

"*Veritas*" is engraved upon the buildings and gates of Harvard University, — "The Truth." Now that the college yard is enclosed by a park fence on every side, this legend from a great Hebrew poet is placed above a principal entrance: — "Open ye the gates that the righteous nation which keepeth truth may enter in." No self-respecting gate upon the globe will open willingly to those who do not keep the truth — "truth in the inward parts," as Hebrew sages used to say, — truth in conscience and life.

Edward Everett Hale relates that, when he was at Harvard, he had the good fortune to be a pupil of Benjamin Pierce for four years. "I shall not forget," he says, "nor will any of the twenty young men who surrounded me, the experience we had one day when

EDWARD EVERETT HALE.

some one had undertaken to copy at the blackboard some memoranda which he had made at home, and which he had privately introduced into the class-room. By some carelessness of his own, his fraud was revealed. In an instant, the whole business of mathematics ceased for that lecture room. Mr. Pierce spoke to us, ashy pale, faltering in voice, on Truth. What was all this study for, but the pursuit of Truth, — if, haply, one could attain it? And here was a creature who pretended to such truth. Pretence in the temple of Truth! A Lie as the work of purity! Truth! None of the twenty men who heard that word of pathetic indignation have forgotten it."

"Mr. Jones," said Ethan Allen, the hero of Ticonderoga, to a lawyer, "I owe a gentleman in Boston sixty pounds on a note, which he has sent to Vermont for collection. I cannot pay it just now, and want you to postpone settlement until I can raise the money."

"All right!" replied Mr. Jones, and when the court next assembled, he arose and said:

"May it please your honor, we deny that this signature is genuine." He knew that this course would require the summoning of witnesses from Boston, which would give Allen all the time he wanted.

"Mr. Jones," shouted Allen, in a voice of thunder, "I did not hire you to come here to lie! This is a true note! I signed it, — I'll swear to it, — and I'll pay it! I want no shuffling. I want time. What I employed you for was to get this matter put over to the next court, not to come here and lie and juggle about it." The lawyer quailed, but the case was put over as Allen wished.

Did you ever think of the blackness of white lies? There are no white lies. They are all black.

Look at the placards in city stores announcing: "Very lowest price," "Discount price," "List price," "Wholesale price," "Half price," "Below cost," "Far below cost of manufacture," "Closing out sale," "Fire sale," "Lowest price ever known," "Reduction sale," "Selling out at cost," "Bankrupt sale," "Assignee's sale," and scores of other lies. Do not go to such stores. If you do, you will be cheated.

"If I hire you," said a Detroit grocer to a boy who had applied for work, "I suppose you will do as I tell you?"

"Yes, sir."

"If I told you to say that the sugar was high grade when it was low, what would you say?"

The boy did not hesitate a moment. "I'd say it," he responded promptly.

"If I told you to say the coffee was pure, when you knew that it had beans in it, what would you say?"

"I'd say it."

"If I told you to say that the butter was fresh, when you knew that it had been in the store for a month, what would you say?"

"I'd say it."

The merchant was nonplussed. "How much will you work for?" he inquired, very seriously.

"One hundred dollars a week," answered the boy, in a business-like tone.

The grocer came near falling from his stool. "One hundred dollars a week?" he repeated, in astonishment.

"With a percentage after the first two weeks," said the boy, coolly. "You see," he went on, "first-class liars come high; and, if you need them in your business, you've got to pay them the price. Otherwise I'll work for three dollars a week." So the boy caught the grocer at his own game and got the job at three dollars a week.

And he never sold a pound of sugar, a pound of coffee, a pound of butter that was not all right; and both grocer and boy prospered in their integrity.

"Truth, unfaltering integrity, justice, and honor are never to be departed from," wrote an eminent American statesman to his son. "Lies come from meanness, low vanity, cowardice, and of a depraved nature, and they always fail of their object and bring the liar into contempt. Without strict integrity, justice, and honor, no one can have continued success in anything, or lasting respect from anybody. Every one is found out sooner or later, and much sooner than he supposes. Indeed, your true character is sure to be known and sure to be justly appreciated."

A man took a seat in a railway car, says a western periodical, and he piled the seat at his side with bags and parcels. The car became crowded, and a gentleman asked if the other half of the seat was occupied. "Yes, those things belong to a man who has just gone into the smoking-car, and he'll be back presently." The gentleman, having reason to suspect the truth of this statement, said, "All right, I will sit here till the man comes back." Proceeding to remove the bundles and bags, he placed them on the floor or in the rack. The other man glared, but could say nothing. As a matter of fact, "the man in the smoking-car" was an invention. By and by the owner of the bundles arrived at his destination, and began to gather up his effects. "Excuse me," said the gentleman, "but you said these bundles belonged to a man in the smoking-car. I shall consider it my duty to prevent you from taking them, since by your own statement they don't belong to you." The man became violent and abusive, but dared not lay his hands on the bundles. The conductor was called in. He listened to the statements of both men, and said: "Well, I will take charge of the bundles myself, and take them to the station in the city; and if no one else claims them meanwhile, you"— indicating the man who had once repudiated their ownership—"may have them." Amid the laughter and applause of the passengers, the man got off at the station, just as the train was pulling out, without his luggage. He obtained it the next day, but was well punished for the lie he had told for the sake of monopolizing a seat that did not belong to him.

Suppose we lived in a world where natural things would lie and deceive us, — a world where the mountains, the sea, the forests, and the rivers were all shams; where the earth, which looks rich and fruitful, would mock us by refusing harvests in return for our seed; where what appears like a beautiful landscape would prove only a deceptive mirage; where gravitation could not be depended upon; where the planets would not keep in their orbits; where the atoms were not true to the law written within them. But it is not so, for there is no sham in nature. It is in regard to man alone that we can say: "Vice has many tools, but a lie is the handle that fits them all."

"It is an old saying," says Margaret Sangster, "that one lie obliges the teller of it to speak half a dozen more, and that before he or she knows it, the situation becomes terribly complicated; but this is not all. The possibility of one's telling a falsehood in any circumstances shows that the character is wanting in perfect integrity or wholeness. I have seen a very beautiful diamond which had lost a great deal of its value because the eye of an expert had found in it a slight flaw. A person who deviates from the truth in the slightest degree has thus produced a flaw in his character. It is something like the little speck in fruit which shows the beginning of decay. Having once persuaded yourself to tell what is not true, you will find it easier the second time to deviate from the truth for some fancied reason."

If a youth should start out with a fixed determination that every statement he makes shall be the exact truth; that every promise he makes shall be redeemed to the letter; that every appointment shall be kept with the strictest faithfulness and with full regard for other men's time; if he should hold his reputation as a priceless treasure, feel that the eyes of the world are upon him, that he must not deviate a hair's breadth from the truth and right; if he should take such a stand at the outset- he would, like George Peabody, come to have almost unlimited credit and the confidence of all; and could have developed into noble man-timber.

Soon after his establishment in Philadelphia, Franklin was offered a piece for publication in his newspaper. Being very busy, he begged the gentleman would leave it for consideration. The next day the author called and asked his opinion of it. " Well, sir," replied Franklin, "I am sorry to say I think it highly scurrilous and defamatory. But being at a loss on account of my poverty as to whether to reject it or not, I thought I would put it to this issue: at night, when my work was done, I bought a two-penny loaf, on which I supped heartily, and then, wrapping myself in my great coat, slept very soundly on the floor until morning, when another loaf and mug of water afforded a pleasant breakfast. Now, sir, since I can live very comfortably in this manner, why should I prostitute my press to personal hatred or party passion for a more luxurious living?"

In our war for the Union, when General Robert E. Lee was in conversation with one of his officers in regard to a movement of his army, a plain farmer's boy overheard the general's remark that he had decided to march upon Gettysburg instead of Harrisburg. The boy telegraphed this fact to Governor Curtin. A special engine was sent for the boy. "I would give my right hand," said the Governor, "to know if this boy tells the truth." A corporal replied: "Governor, I know that boy; it is impossible for him to lie; there is not a drop of false blood in his veins." In fifteen minutes the Union troops were marching to Gettysburg, where they gained a victory. Character is power. The great thing is to be a man, to have a high purpose, a noble aim, to be dead in earnest, to yearn for the good and the true.

Truth, as between man and man in the conduct of business, will never fail if each party will put his conscience into his dealings.

"Trust that man in nothing," said Laurence Sterne, "who has not a conscience in everything." Is not a man who is partly honest, wholly dishonest?

"Put that back," said President John Quincy Adams to his son, who had taken a sheet of paper from a pigeonhole to write a letter. "That belongs to the Government. Here is my own stationery at the other end of the desk. I always use it for letters on private business."

This conscientiousness in regard to what many would consider a mere trifle may appear excessive. But the dividing line between vice and virtue is so fine that the boundary is often unconsciously crossed, and it is just as dangerous for a young person to play at hazards with conscience as it is for a child to toy with a dagger, or to play with fire. He who is honest in small things can be trusted in great.

A nickel is so small a sum that many people think they are not defrauding any one or acting dishonestly if they retain the fare which the street car conductor has forgotten to take. These people would indignantly resent any imputation of dishonesty, yet they have no hesitation in keeping that to which they know they have not the shadow of a right. They would feel themselves injured and defrauded if they knew that their grocer, in weighing tea, or coffee, or any other commodity, had knowingly deprived them of even the most infinitesimal part of their just weight, or that their milkman had held back for his own benefit but one spoonful of the milk for which they had paid. The virtuous indignation of these people against the fraudulent grocer, milkman, or other tradesman, would be fully justified if they themselves observed the Golden Rule. But, if we are not strictly honest ourselves, have we any right to demand or expect that others will be so?

The necessity for absolute integrity in the business world appears from the very nature of the transactions between man and man. The time will never come when men will not have to trust one another in some way. Yet it will always be possible for a man to commit one or two frauds — just as it is now possible for any man to go out with a revolver and kill one or two people whenever he chooses.

"I remember," says Minot J. Savage, "talking with one of the clearest-headed business men in the West I ever knew. He made a claim I was not willing to allow, — that it was honest for him to take advantage of the ignorance of any man with whom he was dealing to get the better end of a bargain. He said that, if he happened to know more than the other man of what was going on in the world, he was justified in taking advantage of the man's ignorance, for he had no one to blame but himself for his ignorance. I question whether that is defensible. Ought we to take advantage of the ignorance, the weakness, the infirmities, the frailties of our fellowmen to leave them worse off than they were before?"

Mark Twain tells us that an impoverished descendant of Audubon, in sore straits, was willing to sell a copy of his great volume on "Birds" for a hundred dollars; it was worth in a market a thousand dollars; the purchaser chuckled over his mean bargain. "How different was Hammond Trumbull," he says. "A lady in the South, in straitened circumstances, wrote him that she had an Eliot's Indian Bible which she would gladly dispose of for a hundred dollars. He wrote to her that, if a perfect copy, it had its market value, one thousand dollars, and he would sell it to the British Museum for that sum. It proved to be such a copy, and she got her thousand dollars in gold. That is the honorable dealing which exalts humanity."

The very least that can be said of a man who cheats his neighbor, through his neighbor's ignorance, is that his character is "out of plumb." We are to use the plumb-line in character-building.

A golden rule for every business man is this: "Put yourself in your customer's place."

I have read a curious story of one. When Philippe Wurtz began to do business for himself it is said he used to kneel and pray over his account book that he might make no entry there that the eye of God would not approve.

Honest money-getting is a timely topic in our modern world. The principle of all right exchange is equivalence, the *quid pro quo*, as the common phrase is. In all honest trade, for every good received, an equivalent good is rendered. In every legitimate bargain both the persons interested are satisfied, and permanently satisfied; each gets what he wants.

Two farmers in Virginia exchanged horses, the condition being that, at the end of a week, the one who thought he had the best bargain should bring the other two bushels of wheat. One week later they met halfway between the two towns each with a bag of wheat. Each thought he had the best bargain. If every one inclined to do a dishonest deed should " put himself in the place " of the other man, and " love him as himself," he would not do it. That is a development of Christianity yet to come.

"No business transaction is honest," says Lyman Abbott, "unless it has for its object the well-being of both parties."

Nathan Straus, the great New York merchant, when asked what had contributed most to his remarkable career, said: "I always looked out for the man at the other end of the bargain."

What a lesson these words contain for the young man of to-day who thinks that long-headedness, shrewdness, cunning, and sharpness are the only success-qualities worth cultivating!

Mr. Straus says that if he got a bad bargain himself he could stand it, even if his losses were heavy, but that he could never afford to have the man who dealt with him get a bad bargain. He felt that his own loss, however great, might possibly be repaired; but that if a man who had dealings with him should lose, or be deceived thereby, nothing could ever compensate him (Mr. Straus) for this, as his character would be permanently injured.

The history of the leading business establishments in this country shows that the men who built them up always looked out for "the man at the other end of the bargain."

One of the most successful grocers in America says he has made it a rule never to have a dissatisfied customer, if it is possible to avoid it, for he feels that such a customer would be a perpetual enemy to his house. Besides, he says, it injures his self-respect to know that any one reasonably lacks confidence in him, because honesty was the foundation stone on which his business was built.

Young men who are in too great a hurry to get rich, who want to build up a successful business in a year or two, without any apprenticeship to the drudgery of details, have their thoughts so selfishly centered on their own aggrandizement that they are very apt to forget "the man at the other end of the bargain."

"Why did you not sell her something?" asked the proprietor as a lady went out of a dry-goods store in Boston without purchasing. "Because," replied the clerk, "she asked for Middlesex, and we did not have it." "Why did you not show her the next pile, and tell her that was Middlesex?" "Because it was not, sir," said the clerk. "You are too mighty particular for me," exclaimed the proprietor. "Very well," said the boy, " if I must tell a lie to keep my place, I will go." The honest clerk became a wealthy, respected merchant in the West.

George Peabody once left a grocery store where he was employed because they sold cigars, declaring he would not sell any man an article which would do him harm.

There is nothing more cruel than the course taken by some employers, which is a constant temptation to employees to be dishonest. Justice Crane, of New York, recently induced an employer to withdraw a charge of theft made against a young man who had stolen an article of small value, and pointed out that the young man's wages — five dollars a week — were a provocation for him to steal. The magistrate thus cited his own experience as a struggling youth in New York City:

"I had to get along on two dollars a week the best way I could. My employers paid no more attention to me than if I had been a dog. I knew that my services were worth at least fifty dollars a week to them, and they paid me two dollars. There were days when I did not eat at all. There was one day — and I shall never forget it — when I was handed two thousand five hundred dollars in cash for my firm when I did not have the price of a meal all day. I confess that, upon that day, only the knowledge that I had a mother who believed in my absolute honesty restrained me from stealing. The firm was one of the largest and most influential in this city. I was pretty near the rock upon which this youth before us foundered, you see."

There is a lesson for every employer in this statement.

To many a man, and sometimes to a youth, there

comes the opportunity to choose between honorable competence and tainted wealth. This is especially true in our large cities, and it is one of the great temptations of our luxurious life. If we could only be content to live in a simple way, as our ancestors did, and as these in the country do, able to look the world in the face because we owe no man a dollar, then there would be less stealing at the till and thieving at the safe. The young man who starts out, willing to be poor and honorable, holds in his hand one of the strongest elements of success.

A Federal colonel, when Vicksburg was taken, says a southern newspaper, had strict orders not to let a bag of cotton go out of the lines. In a short time he had a visit from representatives of some northern cotton mills, and a hint of five thousand dollars was suggested if he would be blind for a time. He cursed the men and ordered them out of his lines, saying: " Do you attempt to bribe me? Leave or I will have you shot." His integrity asserted itself. In a short time he had another visit from those who wanted cotton and a hint of ten thousand dollars suggested. They were cursed and ordered out of the lines. In time a third party visited him and wanted cotton and a hint of twenty thousand was offered. He cursed and ordered them out of the lines. His integrity stood by him so far; but he began to feel troubled in mind. He went to his commanding general and told him of the orders he had received and the temptations offered. Said he: "I want to resign and go home; it is getting most too warm for me. I can stand some things, but not everything. Human nature has its limits, and I am afraid I may find my limit. See here, I was first offered five thousand dollars, then ten, then twenty, and I have stood all that, but the next one who may come along may offer me fifty thousand dollars and I am afraid human nature and self-interest will not be able to stand it. I want to resign and go home before I lose my honor." He saw that if he put his honor and pocketbook in front of him, his pocketbook would win and his honor lose. So he thought it best to get out of the way of opportunity and temptation. Cotton was bringing nearly a dollar per pound at the time.

"Character before wealth," was the motto of Amos Lawrence, who had inscribed on his pocketbook, "What shall it profit a man if he shall gain the whole world and lose his own soul?"

Let me, at this point, go back a moment to the statement I made that the time will never come when men will not have to trust one another in something. It is impossible to do this except upon a common basis.

"There is a point," said Minot J. Savage to his congregation one Sunday, "that I need to call your attention to for a passing moment. I have had occasion to remind you several times during the past years of the fact that this civilized world of ours is only a little way at any time from destitution. If there were no production, if nothing were added to the stock of the world, the world would wear out and eat up all that there is in the course of two or three years, and so perish. Here, then, is this stock of general good; and it seems to me a fundamental principle of business honesty that any man who proposes to take out of this accumulated wealth of the world the tiniest particle for his own use must see to it that he adds something to the general welfare that shall be an equivalent, at least. If he leaves it no richer or if he takes what he has no right to, he becomes, no matter what his position, what we mean by a thief. That is what theft means. Rendering some equivalent, serving the world, adding to its legitimate amusement of welfare in some way, is the only honest condition for any man, woman, or child. Then, when you engage in the world's business, see to it that it is honest, that there is equal exchange. These are the principles that underlie honesty in business.

"Honesty in business, political honesty, religious honesty, honesty in every department of life, — these should be our ideals. We should build not only our houses, but build our social order, our business, our political order, our religious structures of sound materials rightly related to each other, sanely and truly adjusted, so that they will stand, so that they will become a part of the divine order. If we do this, we not only achieve the happiness of other people, the welfare of other people, but, in the long run, we of necessity attain our own happiness and our own welfare, for we cannot possibly live alone. We are dependent every moment of our lives for not only happiness, for not only wealth, but for comfort, for health, for peace upon the general condition of the world in which we are units, of which we are parts. For the sake, then, not only of other people, but also for our own sake, and that we may join hands with God and become a part of His divine order and may help on the perfection of that order which means the kingdom of God, — for the sake of all these things, let us walk honestly."

Not long since, soon after one of the largest defalcations known in the history of American banking, several bank presidents and capitalists in New York made the statement that the only practical protection that the people have for their money is common honesty. All the schemes devised cannot keep criminals from taking what does not belong to them. The best banks in the country have been robbed by the employees who were most trusted. The fact that the wrongdoers had been speculating or living beyond their means came out afterwards, but proved little as to the carefulness of the institution in taking care of the money intrusted to it.

After all is said and done, after every plan has been put in operation, the final safety is common honesty. It is that way in other departments and enterprises of life. Schemes may be invented, bonds may be taken, and efforts may be made to bring honest results, but in the end common honesty is depended upon for protection and for security.

If, therefore, there is anything in your own life which is in the slightest degree at variance with common honesty, you are to that extent an enemy of well-established society, and if all men were like you no society would be possible.

There are men who choose honesty as a soul companion. They live in it, with it, by it. They embody it in their actions and lives. Their words speak it. Their faces beam it. Their actions proclaim it. These are the men who uphold civilization.

"Down on School Street the other day," says a Boston pastor, "a poor Italian took a two and a half dollar gold piece in mistake for a cent. What did he do? Did he hide it away? No. He wrapped it up in a piece of paper and put it where he could give it to the man who had made the mistake, and when he came for it there it was waiting. Was it a trifle? Any of us would trade with that man hereafter, because this tells the story of character, the stuff of which a man is made. When you can break off a little fragment of a man's character, and find it firm and solid, you feel that if he is made of material like that he can be trusted. You have confidence in that kind of stuff and you can build on him. These may be trifles but they make character."

Apart from all question of sentiment there is no doubt of the cash value of business integrity. If civilization is an advantage, in a mercantile point of view, the common honesty which makes civilization possible is an advantage; that is to say, common honesty has a cash value, and a reputation for common honesty is necessary if you expect to succeed in business.

Mayor Hart, of Boston, recently said that in fifty years he has seen the outworking of honesty and fair dealing, that ninety per cent of the successful men have been distinguished for their business integrity, and that those who have taken a counter-course have perished by the way. "Honesty," said he, "is a natural law and the violation of it means retribution, a day of reckoning and punishment. As unerring as the law of gravitation when honesty is violated, it is followed by retribution. The consequences cannot be avoided. They may be deferred but justice must always be faced in the end. A merchant has something that somebody wants, and in return for it he wants that which somebody has. When the trade is effected, if it has been done honestly, both will profit. In the affairs of capital and labor, honesty on both sides must prove advantageous to both. Capital cannot prosper if in its dealings with labor the most rigid honesty is not adhered to; and the rule works the other way as well, just as the experience of ninety per cent of the successful men of the community shows that it works in all affairs of life.

Integrity is the ground of mutual confidence. Upon this ground a youth advances with sure steps. "He is," says Bulwer Lytton, "already of consequence in the world, when it is known that he can be implicitly relied upon."

When Ingram, of the "Illustrated London News," was a young newsdealer, he once walked ten miles to deliver a single paper, rather than disappoint a customer. He could be depended upon, and nothing could hinder him from pushing into the front rank of newspaper men.

What a lesson in honesty is the story of Meyer Anselm, the founder of the great fortune of the Rothschilds, who lived, at the close of the eighteenth century, in that little corner of Frankfort known as Jews' Lane, where his fellow countrymen were terribly persecuted. Even after Napoleon battered down the gates of the city that had locked them in at night and on holidays and Sundays, they were still required to retire at a certain hour, under penalty of death; and they were hounded in a manner which seemed designed to drive them to the lowest condition of life and far from the practice of honest dealings. Anselm, proving an exception to the ordinary ruling character of the Jews around him, established himself in humble quarters, over which he hung a red shield, giving to his family the name of "Rothschild," the German for "red shield." There he conducted the business of a money lender.

When Landgrave William of Hesse-Cassel was driven from his estates by Napoleon, he gathered together five millions of silver, and left it with Anselm, not daring to hope for the possibility of getting it back, for he thought the invaders would surely capture it. The Jew, however, was very shrewd, and, after hiding it in his garden till the danger from the enemy was over, he put it at such interest that, on William's return, Anselm was able to send by his eldest son, to the landgrave's great surprise, a report that the sum loaned, with the usual interest, was at his disposal.

In all the generations of the family, not one member, it is said, has brought a stain upon its business integrity. More than all else, this reputation for sterling honesty is the foundation of the colossal fortune of the Rothschilds.

When A. T. Stewart went into business in New York he determined that the truth should always be told over his counters, whatever the consequences. No clerk was allowed to misrepresent or to cover up a defect. He once asked the opinion of an employee in regard to a large purchase of goods of novel patterns, and was told that the designs were inferior, and some of them in very bad taste. The young man was just pointing out the defects of one particular style, of which he held a sample in his hands, when a large customer from an interior city came up and asked:

"Have you anything new and first-class to show me to-day?"

The young salesman replied promptly, "Yes, sir; we've just brought in something that will suit you to a dot."

Throwing across his arm the very piece he had criticised a moment before, he expatiated upon its beauty so earnestly that a large sale was the result. Mr. Stewart, who had listened in wondering silence, here interrupted, warning the customer to give the goods further and more careful examination, and telling the young man to call upon the cashier for any wages due him, as his final account would be made up at once.

Stewart's integrity paid, and paid in cash. "In building up a business the grandest advertisement ever written is poor compared with a reputation for keeping honest goods and telling the exact truth about them. Found your business on truth, and the superstructure will be a success."

Wedgwood, the potter, although he rose from a workman, was never satisfied till he had done his best. He would tolerate no inferior work. If it did not come up to his idea of what it should be, he would break the vessel, and throw it away, saying, "That won't do for Josiah Wedgwood." Character makes reputation; and the Wedgwood pottery, with Wedgwood's honesty behind it, won world-wide celebrity.

When Lincoln became a lawyer, all clients knew that they would win if the case was a fair one; and, if not, that it was a waste of time to take it to him. After listening some time, with his eyes on the ceiling, one day to a would-be client's statement, he swung suddenly round in his chair and exclaimed:

"Well, you have a pretty good case in technical law, but a pretty bad one in equity and justice. You'll have to get some other fellow to win this case for you. I could n't do it. All the time, while standing talking to that jury, I'd be thinking, 'Lincoln, you're a liar,' and I believe I should forget myself and say it out loud."

After giving considerable time to a case in which he had received from a lady a retainer of two hundred dollars, he returned the money, saying: "Madam, you have not a peg to hang your case on." "But you have earned that money," said the lady. "No, no," replied Lincoln, "that would not be right. I can't take pay for doing my duty."

He refused to argue a case when he learned that his client had deceived him by representing that his cause was just. His partner, however, took the case, and won it, receiving a fee of nine hundred dollars, of which Lincoln refused to take his half.

His integrity came at length to be bone of his bone, and flesh of his flesh; and no one could meet him or hear him without knowing he was honest. "I won't hear him," exclaimed a man, as he left the hustings where Lincoln was speaking in 1856, "for I don't like a man that makes me believe in him in spite of myself."

When an attempt was made to secure the passage of an ordinance of repudiation in Illinois, Stephen A. Douglas lay ill at a hotel in Springfield. He asked to be carried to the convention; and while lying upon his mattress, wrote as a substitute for the repudiation bill:

"*Resolved*, That Illinois will be honest, although she never pays a cent."

It was adopted, and was the deathblow to repudiation, not only in Illinois but also in all the other States. The credit and prosperity of the whole nation rose at once.

In 1837, after George Peabody moved to London, there came a commercial crisis in the United States. Many banks suspended specie payments. Many mercantile houses went to the wall, and thousands more were in great distress. Edward Everett said, "The great sympathetic nerve of the commercial world, credit, as far as the United States were concerned, was for the time

BUSINESS INTEGRITY.

paralyzed." Probably not a half-dozen men in Europe would have been listened to for a moment in the Bank of England upon the subject of American securities, but George Peabody was one of them. His name was already a tower of strength in the commercial world. In those dark, dark days his integrity stood four-square in every business panic. Peabody retrieved the credit of the State of Maryland, and, it might almost be said, of the United States. His character was the magic wand which in many a case changed almost worthless paper into gold. Merchants on both sides of the Atlantic procured large advances from him, even before the goods consigned to him had been sold.

When Walter Scott's publisher and printer failed and six hundred thousand dollars of debt stared them in the face, friends came forward and offered to raise money enough to allow him to arrange with his creditors. "No," said he proudly, "this right hand shall work it all off; if we lose everything else we will at least keep our honor unblemished." What a grand picture of manliness, of integrity in this noble man, working like a dray-horse to cancel that great debt, throwing off at white heat the "Life of Napoleon," "Woodstock," "The Tales of a Grandfather," articles for the "Quarterly," and so on, all written in the midst of great sorrow, pain, and ruin. "I could not have slept soundly," he writes, "as I now can under the comfortable impression of receiving the thanks of my creditors and the conscious feeling of discharging my duty as a man of honesty. I see before me a long, tedious, and dark path, but it leads to stainless reputation. If I die in the harness, as is very likely, I shall die with honor."

Samuel L. Clemens (Mark Twain), one of the world's

best known and best loved men, has added a new chapter to the story of honesty between man and man, by making one more "tramp abroad" to pay his debts. He went around the world this time to satisfy his conscience. The great humorist's example has afforded an inspirational example to all debt-ridden countrymen. At first we simply laughed at Twain's jokes. Then we discovered that they are literature. Next we learned, against our will, that the humorist is something else, — a serious soul, who does not love the laughter he provokes. At length, the humorist turns out to be one of the most striking examples of the honesty of his country, a quality that the world has tried to deny to all jokers. Here is a man who can exemplify his country's gift of humor and its honor at the same time.

Possibly the greatest test of honesty is found in the rare instances of paying debts long after they have been outlawed. Considerations of policy influence most men to be honest, while conscience pricks some into restoring what has been wrongfully withheld. But where a man has been released from his debts, and then volunteers to pay them, the example is inspiring.

Bolton Hall, an attorney and tax reformer, a son of the celebrated divine, Dr. John Hall, recently paid off one hundred thousand dollars of released debt, impelled solely by honor.

Is not business integrity a valuable asset? Were the thousands of business men, who lost every dollar they had in the Chicago fire, enabled to go into business again at once, some into wholesale business, without money? Their record for honesty became their bank account. The commercial agencies said they were square men;

SAMUEL L. CLEMENS.
(Mark Twain)

that they had always paid one hundred cents on a dollar; that they had paid promptly, and that they were industrious and dealt honorably with all men. They drew on their character. Character was the coin which enabled penniless men to buy thousands of dollars' worth of goods. Their integrity did not burn up with their stores. The best part of them was beyond the reach of fire and could not be burned.

"Thousands of dollars are loaned on character," said a St. Louis bank president at a recent convention of bankers; "for there are men of such high character — though not rich in this world's goods — that they will not borrow more than they can pay." That was the reply he made when he was asked concerning the ability of small capitalists — men doing a small business — to raise money on credit. Another banker put it more bluntly, saying that he would rather lend money to an honest poor man than to a rich knave who could give substantial security. The tenor of all the replies was a tribute of hard-headed business men to the great value of a business reputation for honesty. It was a striking evidence of the fact that proved integrity is business capital, and that such capital is within reach of every man.

"A dozen men," said a well-known business man to a youth just starting in business, "will sell you an outfit on credit because they know you. Poverty, with such a character as you have, is better capital than ten thousand dollars would be to some men." "Every young man comes in contact with chances for money-making," says a prominent merchant. "To use them, he must have friends who have learned to rely on his honesty and judgment. Such friendships are only made through the medium of a carefully cultivated reputation for integrity of purpose."

If any young man proposes to conduct any kind of business it is of the utmost importance for him to know, at the outset, that the mercantile world is "business-like" and systematic, and that merchants act upon the principle of keeping tally. Everything counts. Commercial agencies record every movement made from the time one enters business. If not fair and upright in all your dealings, you will be greatly hampered; if honest and trustworthy, your credit may in time be unlimited. Creditors will have nothing to do with a person tricky and unscrupulous; merchants and bankers extend credit according to their confidence.

Merchants have the best fraud police. They have their regular detective agencies in their Duns and Bradstreets; they have their private detectives in the shape of their credit men. They also have credit guaranty companies, — a modern invention. The most minute information is recorded by the mercantile agencies. The nature of the business, its details, and the life-stories of the partners, their ability, habits, and character are all given.

All these precautions are not an absolute protection against fraudulent men, but they do protect against men who continue to be fraudulent. No one can visit one of the great business agencies without being impressed with the magnitude of their recording work. Every business man's record is either for him or against him.

XXXI.

WRESTING TRIUMPH FROM DEFEAT.

"I WISH," said President Roosevelt, in a recent address in Washington, "to see in the average American citizen the determination not to shrink back when temporarily beaten in life, as each will be now and then, but to come up again and *wrest triumph from defeat.*"

"To come up again and wrest triumph from defeat." That is the secret of the success of every brave and noble life that ever was lived.

Perhaps the past has been a bitter disappointment to you. In looking it over you may feel that you have been a failure, or at best have been plodding along in mediocrity. You may not have succeeded in the particular things you expected to do; you may have lost money when you expected to make it; or you may have lost friends and relatives who were very dear to you. You may have lost your business, and even your home may have been wrenched from you because you could not pay the mortgage on it, or because of sickness and consequent inability to work. A serious accident may have apparently robbed you of power. The New Year may present a very discouraging outlook to you. Yet, in spite of any or all of these misfortunes, if you refuse to be conquered, victory is awaiting you farther on the road.

A little boy was asked how he learned to skate. "Oh, by getting up every time I fell down," he replied. This is the spirit that leads men and armies to victory. It is not the fall but the not getting up that is defeat.

After twelve thousand of Napoleon's soldiers had been overwhelmed by the advance of seventy-five thousand Austrian troops, he addressed them thus: "I am displeased with you. You have evinced neither discipline nor valor. You have allowed yourselves to be driven from positions where a handful of resolute men might have arrested an army. You are no longer French soldiers. Chief of Staff, cause it to be written on their standards, '*They are no longer of the army of Italy.*'"

In tears the battered veterans replied: "We have been misrepresented. The soldiers of the enemy were three to one. Try us once more. Place us in the post of danger and see if we do not belong to the army of Italy." In the next battle they were placed in the van, and they made good their pledge by rolling back the great Austrian army.

He is a pretty poor sort of man who loses courage and fears to face the world just because he has made a mistake or a slip somewhere, because his business has failed, because his property has been swept away by some general disaster, or because of other trouble impossible for him to avert.

This is the test of your manhood: how much is there left in you after you have lost everything outside of yourself? If you lie down now, throw up your hands, and acknowledge yourself worsted, there is not much in you. But if, with heart undaunted and face turned forward, you refuse to give up or to lose faith in yourself, if you scorn to beat a retreat, you will show that the man left in you is bigger than your loss, greater than your cross, and larger than any defeat.

"I know no such unquestionable badge and ensign of a sovereign mind," said Emerson, "as that tenacity of purpose which, through all changes of companions, or parties, or fortunes, changes never, bates no jot of heart or hope, but wearies out opposition and arrives at its port."

It is men like Ulysses S. Grant, who, whether in the conflict of opposing armies on the battlefield, or in the wear and tear of civic strife, fighting against reverses, battling for a competence for his loved ones, even while the hand of death lay chill upon him, "bates no jot of heart or hope," that wring victory from the most forbidding circumstances. It is men like Napoleon, who refuse to recognize defeat, who declare that "impossible" is not in their vocabularies, that accomplish things.

You may say that you have failed too often, that there is no use in trying, that it is impossible for you to succeed, and that you have fallen too often even to attempt to get on your feet again. Nonsense! There is no failure for a man whose spirit is unconquered. No matter how late the hour or how many and repeated his failures, success is still possible. The evolution of Scrooge, the miser, in the closing years of his life, from a hard, narrow, heartless money-grubber, whose soul was imprisoned in his shining heap of hoarded gold, to a generous, genial lover of his kind, is no mere myth of Dickens' brain. Time and again in the history of our daily lives, chronicled in our newspapers, recorded in biographies, or exhibited before our eyes, we see men and women redeeming past failures, rising up out of the stupor of discouragement, and boldly turning face forward once more.

There are thousands of people who have lost everything they had in the world who are just as far from failure as they were before their loss, because of their unconquerable spirit, — stout hearts that never quail. How much we owe to this great army of the invincible which is forever amongst us wringing victory from defeat!

There can be no failure to a man who has not lost his courage, his character, his self-respect, or his self-confidence. He is still a king.

If you are made of the stuff that wins, if you have grit and nerve in you, your misfortunes, losses, and defeats will call them out and make you all the stronger. "It is defeat," says Beecher, "that turns bone to flint and gristle to muscle and makes men invincible."

Some people get along beautifully for half a lifetime, perhaps, while everything goes smoothly. While they are accumulating property and gaining friends and reputation their characters seem to be strong and well-balanced; but the moment there is friction anywhere — the moment trouble comes, a failure in business, a panic, or a great crisis in which they lose their all — they are overwhelmed. They despair, lose heart, courage, faith, hope and power to try again, — everything. Their manhood or womanhood is swallowed up by a mere material loss.

This is failure, indeed, and there is small hope for any one who falls to such a depth of despair. There is hope for an ignorant man who cannot write his name, even, if he has stamina and backbone. There is hope for a cripple who has courage; there is hope for a boy who has nerve and grit, even though he is so hemmed in that he has apparently no chance in the world, but there is no hope for a man who cannot or will not stand up after he falls, but loses heart when opposition strikes him, and lays down his arms after defeat.

Let everything else go, if you must, but never lose your grip on yourself. Do not let your manhood or womanhood go. This is your priceless pearl, dearer to you than your breath. Cling to it with all your might. Give up life itself first.

A man should be so much greater than any material failure that can come to him that it would scarcely be mentioned in his biography, and that it would be regarded as a mere incident in his career — inconvenient but not very important. In true manhood there is something which rises higher than worldly success or failure. No matter what reverses come to him, what disappointments or failures, a really great man rises superior to them. He never loses his equanimity. In the midst of storms and trials to which a weak nature would succumb, his serene soul, his calm confidence still assert themselves, so completely dominating all outward conditions that they have no power to harm him. Like a great monarch of the forest, amid the war of elements he stands unshaken through all changes and ravages of time.

I have been in the track of a terrible tornado the day after it had swept on its path of destruction. It had uprooted everything that was weak, and had twisted off every tree that was rotten at heart or that was not firm of fiber. Only the stalwart and true, those that were sound to the core, withstood the awful test. All the buildings in a village through which I passed, except the strongest, whose foundations were deep and firm, went down before its terrible force. When the great historic panics swept over this country the weak houses, with small capital, or headed by men without great resources of experience and character went down by thousands. Only the sound and vigorous, with great reserves of power and capital, withstood the ordeal. Little, weak, backboneless, nerveless men are the first to go down when an emergency comes, and hard times and panics frighten capital. Obstacles paralyze the weak, but strengthen the strong.

"What is defeat?" says Wendell Phillips. "Nothing but the first steps to something higher." Many a one has finally succeeded only because he has failed after repeated efforts. If he had never met defeat he would never have known any great victory. There is something in defeat which puts new determination into a man of mettle. He, perhaps, would be content to go along in comparative mediocrity but for the stimulus of failure. This rouses him to do his best. He comes to himself after some stinging defeat, and perhaps for the first time feels his real power, like a horse who takes the bit in his mouth and runs away for the first time when he had previously thought that he was a slave of his master.

A great many people never really discover themselves until ruin stares them in the face. They do not seem to know how to bring out their reserves until they are overtaken by an overwhelming disaster, or until the sight of their blighted prospects and of the wreck of their homes and happiness stirs them to the very center of their beings.

Young men who never amounted to much, when suddenly overtaken by some great sorrow or loss, or other misfortune, have developed a power for self-assertion, for aggressiveness, an ability to grapple with the difficulty or trouble confronting them which they never before dreamed they possessed, and of which no one who knew them conceived them capable. The very desperation of the situation spurred them on to do what they would not have thought possible in their former ease and luxury. They had never touched their power before and did not know their strength until the emergency came.

Many a girl who has been reared in luxury and ease, who has never had practical training, is suddenly thrown upon her own resources by the death of her father, or the loss of property, and instead of being cared for, nursed and caressed by tender parents, she finds herself obliged, not only to support herself, but also to take care of brothers and sisters and an invalid mother. This crisis which confronts her calls out her reserve and develops an independence and power of self-effort which no one ever imagined she possessed, and which is amazing even to herself.

There is a certain something in our nature, a divine force, which we cannot describe or explain, which does not seem to inhere in any of our ordinary faculties, which lies deeper than any visible attribute, but which rushes to our assistance in great emergencies, in supreme crises. When death or danger threatens in railroad or steamship accidents how often we see men, and sometimes frail women, exert the power of giants in their efforts to extricate themselves from the impending peril. In disasters at sea, during the great fires or floods, how often have delicate girls and women performed Herculean tasks, tasks which they would have deemed impossible had it not been for the magic stimulus born of the emergency.

It is the locked-up spiritual forces within us — forces that we do not, as a rule, call to our aid in the ordinary experiences of life — that make men giants, that stamp humanity with the divine seal. The man who uses all the resources that the Divine Power has implanted with him cannot fail. It would be strange, indeed, if the grandest of God's creatures were ever, in his real character, at the mercy of the accidents which make and unmake fortunes. No, there is no failure for the man who realizes his power, who never knows when he is beaten; there is no failure for the determined endeavor; the unconquerable will. There is no failure for the man who gets up every time he falls, who rebounds like a rubber ball, who persists when every one else gives up, who pushes on when every one else turns back.

"SOMETHING WHICH BRINGS THINGS OUT RIGHT IN SPITE OF ME."

How many times we come to a crisis in life when some obstacle confronts us which we think will be a terrible calamity and will perhaps ruin us if we cannot avoid it. We fear that our ambition will be thwarted, or that our lives, perhaps, will be wrecked. The dread of the shock which we think will overwhelm us as we come nearer and nearer to it, without any possibility of averting it, is something frightful.

Many a time in the writer's life has he come to such a point, — when it seemed as if all was lost, — and yet something beyond his control has straightened out the tangle, solved the puzzle which seemed insoluble; the storm which threatened shipwreck has passed over, the sun has come out again, and everything has become tranquil and serene once more. If we look ahead, the troubles seem thick and threatening, but when we get there we usually find a clear path, plenty of room, pleasant faces, and people to help us in case of need. When we look back over our lives how few accidents have really happened to us. Many have threatened, but, somehow, things have come out right in spite of us, so that we have wasted our vitality, we have grown old and wrinkled and bent, and have shortened our youth anticipating troubles and worrying about calamities which never were to happen. Why should we thus needlessly throw away happiness and usefulness?

It seems strange that when we know perfectly well that we are dependent for every breath we draw upon a Divine Power which is constantly providing for us and protecting us, we do not learn to trust it with absolute confidence and resignation.

There is only one thing for us to do, and that is to do our level best right where we are every day of our lives; to use our best judgment, and then to trust the rest to that Power which holds the forces of the universe in His hand and which does all things well.

XXXII.

OIL YOUR MENTAL MACHINERY.

"PREPARE yourself for the world," said Lord Chesterfield, "as the athletes used to do for their exercises: oil your mind and your manners to give them the necessary suppleness and flexibility; strength alone will not do it."

To thus keep one's self supple and flexible in mind and body and manners is to keep constantly growing. Chesterfield had in mind an ideal social success merely when he spoke of the necessity of keeping mind and manners supple and flexible by oiling. But the business man, the professional man, the scholar, the writer, the teacher, the preacher, or any other man who desires to advance in his calling must keep his mental machinery constantly oiled. If he does not, he cannot hope to retain his suppleness and flexibility or the susceptibility to new ideas upon which progress depends and the foundation of industry is built.

In the early days of our history, when the roads of Nantucket Island were few, and those not of the best, notices were posted at various points on the sandy plains, warning passengers not to "rut the road." "The evident idea," says a recent writer, "was that you would make better progress yourself and be more considerate of others, if you would take a fresh path each time you went over the plain, instead of going again and again in the same tracks."

We all know the danger of falling into ruts. If it is not literally true that "familiarity breeds contempt," there can be no doubt that in many instances long familiarity with our surroundings makes us insensible to their defects. If the mind is not kept flexible and thoroughly responsive to new ideas, by means of contact with other minds; if it is not kept alive by constant effort to reach the highest ideals formed in youth, not only will a man's business, his trade, profession, or occupation suffer, but the whole man will also gradually deteriorate. The brain, like the muscles of the body, grows only by use. As soon as a man ceases to exercise his highest faculties in the pursuit of his chosen work, both his brain and his work lose little by little until he ceases to be able to measure himself by other men or to judge of his work or business from an unprejudiced standpoint. When he has reached this stage growth is at an end; deterioration has already made rapid strides.

Nothing is more conducive to progress and more helpful in keeping one up to high standards than taking one's bearings now and then, and making, as it were, a fresh start. Whatever a man's occupation or profession may be, his chances of attaining marked success in it are ten to one if he makes up his mind at the outset that, at least once a year, he will make a thorough study of himself and his methods from the standpoint of an outsider.

It is easy to promise ourselves, when starting out in life, that we will never lower our ideals, that we will always go onward and upward, and that we will ever be found abreast of our times in sympathy and coöperation with the leaders of progressive thought. We do not dream of the constant vigilance that must be exercised in order to keep our ideals in sight; we do not count on all the influences from without and within against which we must struggle if we would remain true to the high and beautiful aspirations of youth.

The only way to be happy is to take advantage of the little opportunities that come to us to brighten life as we go along. To postpone enjoyment day after day, and year after year, until we get more money or a better position, the means to travel or buy works of art, to build an elegant mansion, or to attain some distant goal of ambition, is to cheat ourselves not only of present enjoyment, but also of the power to enjoy in the future.

Speaking of looking forward to happiness, some one had aptly said: "I would as soon chase butterflies for a living or bottle moonshine for a cloudy night." Postponed enjoyment is always a failure. Many young married people, starting out with little capital, work like slaves for years, putting aside every opportunity for pleasure or relaxation, denying themselves the luxury of an occasional outing, attendance at a theater or concert, a trip to the country or the purchase of a coveted book, and postponing even their reading and general culture until they shall have more leisure and more money. Each year they promise themselves that by the following year they will be ready to take life easier, perhaps to indulge in a little travel. When the next year comes, however, they feel that they must economize a while longer. Thus they put off their enjoyment from year to year, scarcely realizing the import of the fact that each successive postponement causes less pain than the previous one.

At length the time comes when they decide that they

can afford to indulge in a little pleasure. Perhaps they go abroad, or they try to enjoy music and works of art, or attempt to broaden their minds by reading and study. But it is too late. They have become hopelessly wedged into the rut the years have made for them. The freshness of life has departed. Enthusiasm has fled. The fire of ambition is dead. The long years of waiting have crushed the capacity to enjoy. The possessions for which they have sacrificed all their natural and healthy longings for joy and brightness have turned to Dead Sea fruits.

Such lives, which are repeated in thousands of homes all about us, are almost worthless. They contribute little to the sum of human happiness and progress. Such living is no real life; it is only existence.

Has life no higher meaning than to draw in the breath and blow it out again? Has it no broader significance than that indicated by the dollar mark, or by lands, houses, and a big bank account? Why did the Creator make us in His image and put within us marvelous powers if they are to be mocked or allowed to die without development or satisfaction? If man is to live like a brute, why does he bear the human form, the impress of divinity?

Aspiration for enjoyment and longing for brightness and happiness were not implanted in us without a purpose. They were meant to play their part in our unfoldment, just as truly as ambition, desire for knowledge, or beauty, or virtue, or any of the other nobler qualities of mankind. As a rule, the man who cultivates a habit of enjoyment, who gladly avails himself of the opportunity each day offers to indulge in some innocent pleasure, to brighten and broaden his life by listening to good music, looking at rare works of art, studying the beauties of nature, or reading an inspiring book, will, unconsciously, find himself far ahead in the race for success of the one who postpones all his enjoyment and relaxation until he has accumulated a fortune.

XXXIII.

THE MAN WHO COULD N'T AFFORD A VACATION.

No man or woman can work every day, year in and year out, with no change, no variety in his life, without either getting into a rut which will paralyze his finest and best faculties, or breaking down altogether and shortening years of precious life.

A great many people, especially in cities, fail, lose their health, and become mere apologies of the men and women they might be if they knew how to take care of themselves, — if they were wise enough to take a vacation when they need it. But they voluntarily cut themselves off, year after year, from the great source of power, — nature. They do not drink from the fountain of vitality and eternal youth and energy in which the earth is constantly renewing itself. Buried in schemes of ambition, of self-aggrandizement, in dreams of wealth and power and fame, they grind away in an environment of bricks and mortar, in the stifling, changeless atmosphere of the city, until they become nervous, worn-out wrecks. They do not see the necessity of change; they do not believe in taking a vacation; they laugh at the idea of giving up their work and going away to idle in the country, as they put it, until it is too late. Many of these ceaseless toilers are living on their nerves, trying all sorts of patent medicines, massage treatments, and other artificial remedies, in the hope of regaining health and strength. But they find these things very poor substitutes for the recreating rejuvenating forces of the country.

How much money would you give a physician if he would guarantee you strong, steady, healthy faculties, instead of nervous, exhausted ones; if he could restore elasticity to your lagging footsteps; if he could give you firm, vigorous muscles instead of weak, flabby ones; if he could put new courage and hope into your life; if he could, by some magic, take away the fretful, nervous, irritable feeling which makes you so unhappy, and restore you to your usual cool, calm, collected, cheerful demeanor? You would not stop at any price you could afford to pay. Yet you can do all this yourself if you will only drop everything and fly to the country for rest and change and complete emancipation from business cares. Let your business for the time be to recuperate and to grow strong.

A great many business and professional men are practically slaves to their vocation. They are a part of its machinery. They have become victims of routine. They do what they do to-day because they did it yesterday. It is easier to go back to the accustomed task than to make a change of any kind, no matter how much they may need it.

I have lived for years near a man who says he never could afford to take a vacation. I have called at his office a great many times, but have never found him at leisure; he is always on the grind; there is no let up in his work from one year's end to another; he believes in the gospel of hard, unremitting work for himself and everybody around him. He says that all this talk about rest and vacation is nonsense; that time taken from business is time wasted; that life is too short for one to go out into the country and sit around doing nothing.

The result is that his close application to work through all these years has broken down his health. His hand trembles so that he can scarcely sign a check. His once vigorous, firm step has given way to an uncertain, lagging one, and there are evidences of weakness in his very bearing. He gives you the impression of a man who is just about to collapse, yet he refuses to give up work or to take a vacation. Although the man has made money, he is a complete failure. No one who works for him sympathizes with him, because they think he is too mean and stingy to take a rest. His family, as well as his employees, avoid him, because he has become so crabbed and disagreeable. He is a mere business machine — hard, cold, and unresponsive to human emotions. If one were to show him a picture of himself as he really is — as the years of grind and drudgery have made him — he would not believe it was a true one. He thinks he is the same free, open-hearted, generous fellow that he was in his youth.

Everywhere we see duplicates of this man who could not afford to take a vacation. He is listlessly dragging his feet along the streets, trying, now and then, to force himself, by sheer will-power, to express energy which he does not possess. We see him at home — fretful, irritable, morose — pushing away from the children whom he once loved to caress and play with. He cannot bear their noise, or enter into their childish fun. He tries to get away in a corner by himself, with his paper or book. He feels injured because he thinks his wife does not make as much of him as she used to. He does not realize that in his nervous moodiness he has repelled her loving attentions and caresses so often that she shrinks from repeating them. All unconsciously, he is severing the tenderest ties of his family life, and making his home miserable.

We finally see this man, who once imagined he could not afford to take a vacation, at foreign resorts, drinking the waters and taking mud baths. We see him at hot springs, sulphur springs — all sorts of mineral springs — trying to recover what he bartered for a mess of pottage. He is taking long trips in automobiles; he is on steamships and yachts seeking health on the ocean; he is traveling from place to place, consulting the world's great specialists, trying to get back the vigor and vitality he lost in exchange for the money he made while toiling along year after year without rest or change.

The brain will very quickly tell you when it needs a vacation. When it demands a change, it will give you signs that cannot be mistaken. It will humiliate you often enough, and make you wonder whether or not you are a real man or woman, when you lose your self-control and fly into a rage over the merest trifles; when you have to force yourself to the work that was formerly a delight; when you begin to feel dull and languid and irritable; when your ambition and enthusiasm begin to wane; when your head aches, your eye loses its luster, and your step its elasticity. Whether you are a student, a business or professional man or woman, or a homemaker, these are symptoms which you cannot afford to ignore. They are Nature's reminders that you must stop, or take the consequences. If you do not heed her warnings she will make you pay the penalty, though it be with your life. Whether king or beggar, it is all the same to her. Beware how you presume to do what Nature prohibits. She will warn you once, twice, thrice, perhaps oftener, but from her final sentence there is no appeal.

Many a man has been carried to his rest in a hearse years before his natural span of life was run, because he put off his vacation until he could afford the time. Others are in hospitals, sanitariums, and asylums, helpless wrecks from *paresis*, over-taxed brains, shattered nerves, or broken down constitutions, because they thought they could not afford a few weeks' vacation every year.

We notice that the men who tell you they cannot get out of harness even for a week, because their business or profession presses them so, are not, as a rule, as good business men, and do not succeed as well in their professions, as the men who take time to recuperate and grow. There have been great changes in business methods in the past twenty-five years. The more progressive men, those who are capable of making and carrying out a programme in a large way, have broken away from the old slavery of their predecessors. They do not spend as many hours in the office, but they can do more and better work in less time, because they have better facilities; they are fresher and more spontaneous, because their faculties are not jaded and worn out by long hours of drudgery.

When will men learn that power does not come from bricks and stones and artificial environment? If we would gain in force and originality, we must go back to a simpler life. We have become too artificial. We must touch mother earth. We must drink in power from the babbling brook, from the meadow, from the mountain. We must drink in beauty from flower and field, and tree and sunset, or we shall go backward instead of forward. Growth and power, strength and efficiency must be our aim. To do our best, we must be healthy, strong. If we grind incessantly, this is impossible.

DOES IT PAY?

Does it pay to regain your cheerful personality?

Does it pay to sip power from its very fountain head?

Does it pay to increase your creative power and originality?

Does it pay to get a firmer grip on your business or profession?

Does it pay to regain your lost confidence by up-building your health?

Do you want to get rid of the scars and stains of the year's campaign?

Will a fresh, vigorous brain serve you better than a fagged, jaded one?

Does it pay to exchange flaccid, stiffened muscles for strong, elastic ones?

Does it pay to get a new grip upon life and to double your power to do good work?

Does it pay to put iron into the blood and to absorb granite strength from the everlasting hills?

Does it pay to renew the buoyancy and light-heartedness, the spontaneity and enthusiasm of youth?

Does it pay to get in tune with the Infinite .by drinking in the medicinal tonic from the everlasting hills?

Does it pay to get rid of your nagging, rasping disposition so that you can attract people instead of repelling them?

Does it pay to get rid of some of our narrow prejudices, hatreds, and jealousies that are encouraged by the strenuous city life?

Does it pay to add to the comfort and happiness of ourselves and those about us by being brighter and more cheerful ourselves?

Does it pay to make the most of all the powers that God has given you by bringing superb health and vitality to your aid in developing them?

Does it pay to develop our powers of observation; to learn to read " books in the running brooks, sermons in stones, and good in everything ? "

Does it pay to put beauty into the life, to gather serenity and poise from the sweet music of the running brooks and the thousand voices in nature?

Is it better to be a full-rounded man or woman with large views and a wide outlook, or a mere automatic machine running in the same old grooves year after year?

Is it a good investment to exchange a few dollars for a great deal of health and happiness; to economize on that which the very wellsprings of our being depend?

Does it pay to be free, for a time, from the petty annoyances that vex, hinder, and exasperate; to get out of ruts and the old beaten tracks and take in a stock of brand-new ideas?

Does it pay to get away from the hot bricks and mortar of the city and breathe the pure air of the country; to become rejuvenated and refreshened by breathing the untainted and invigorating air of the country?

Is it better to go to your task with a hopeful outlook than to drag yourself to your work like an unwilling slave; to go through life halting, weak, inefficient, pessimistic, or to be strong, vigorous, self-reliant and optimistic?

Does it pay to save five per cent of your income by economizing on your vacation this year and break down next year from the continued strain and be obliged to pay fifty per cent. for doctor's bills, besides the time lost in enforced idleness?

Does it pay the hard-worked, nerve-racked, desk-bound man to lock his business cares in his office or store and be free once more; to exchange exhausted and irritable nerves for sound, healthy ones, which will carry pleasurable sensations instead of rasping ones?

XXXIV.

FRESHNESS IN WORK.

FRESHNESS gives an indescribable flavor to our work, whatever it may be. It does not matter how able a book is, if it has not the charm of originality and spontaneity; if we see in it the marks of great effort or straining for effect, we do not care for it; it does not hold our attention. It is the same with a picture, a statue, a song, or a poem, — a work of any kind. If it lacks originality, we will have none of it. But, if the book, the picture, or the poem is vigorous and spontaneous, if it throbs with life, if it has the freshness and fragrance of new-mown hay, or of flowers just opened, we enjoy it with our whole souls.

The great trouble with many people's work is that it is stale, labored, and heavy. It lacks vitality, vivacity; it bears evidence of a depleted mind and an exhausted body. It is easy to trace the tired feeling which an author has dragged all through the pages of his book. It can be seen in the imperfect combinations of color, the tameness and lack of life in the figures upon the canvas of the worn-out artist. The results of an overworked brain, or a brain that is weakened by vicious living, are all marked with the fatal stamp of inferiority.

It makes all the difference in the world, in results, whether you come to your work every day with all your powers intact, with all your faculties up to the standard; whether you come with the entire man, so that you can fling your whole life into your task, or with only a part of yourself; whether you do your work as a giant or as a pigmy. Most people bring only a small part of themselves to their tasks. They cripple much of their ability by irregular living, bad habits in eating, injurious food, and lack of sleep. They do not come to their tasks every morning whole men; a part of themselves, and often a large part, is somewhere else. They were trying to have a good time. They bring weakness instead of power, indifference and dulness instead of enthusiasm and alertness, to the performance of the most important duties of their lives. The man who comes to his work in the morning unrefreshed, languid, and listless cannot do a good, honest day's work, and, if he drags rotten days into the year, how can he expect a sound career or a successful achievement?

Good work is not entirely a question of will-power, — often this is impaired by a low physical standard. The quality of the work cannot be up to high-water mark when every faculty, every function, and every bit of your ability is affected by your physical and mental condition. You may be sure that your weakness, whatever its cause, will appear in your day's work, whether it is making books or selling them, teaching school or studying, singing or painting, chiseling statues or digging trenches.

Beauty is a child of freshness. No artist with ebbing force, with his mental and physical powers exhausted, can produce any work that will please or live. No worker in art, in literature, or in any field of effort, can greatly benefit the world if he is not in a condition to do strong, fresh work, stamped with the power of his own individuality.

Many writers, artists, and musicians — persons in all walks of life — have wondered at their waning popularity, when those who knew them could see the deterioration in their work, and its cause, in the dropping ideal, the letting down of standards, the failure to keep themselves fresh, vigorous, and strong. A man might as well wonder why his horse, which he has been riding all day, without rest, food, or water, and goading with whip and spur, should lag in speed or not feel as supple, elastic, and fresh in the evening as when he started out in the morning.

What should we think of a great singer who, after a night of dissipation, should work hard all day, go without food, sleep or rest, and yet expect to appear before the public the same evening and achieve a triumph in the most difficult rôle she had ever attempted? We should surely think she must be insane. We should expect that any woman of ordinary common sense would do everything in her power to keep her physical and mental condition up to the highest point of excellence for such an occasion. We should expect that she would take care to get all the sleep and rest possible, that she would avoid excitement, worry, and every form of mental and physical dissipation which would sap her energies or reduce her vitality, so that she might come to her task with all the freshness, spontaneity, and enthusiasm possible.

This is what we should naturally look for from any one preparing for any important task. It is fresh faculties — fresh brain, nerve, and muscle cells — that do fresh strong work, work which has the flavor of immortality. When the vitality is low, when the faculties are jaded, when hope has hauled down her flag, and despair and *melancholia* are in the ascendant, we can produce nothing that will live! There is no immortality in our work. Death is written all over it.

It is a man's duty to keep all his powers up to such a standard that he can fling himself into his task with all the freshness and enthusiasm of which he is capable. Then his work will spell something; his life will have a meaning.

Had one the power to analyze the cause of his non-success, many a failure could see these things standing out all over his career, — insufficient sleep, lack of exercise in the open air, lack of change and recreation, irregularity and want of system in his method of living.

The youth who would get the most out of life, who would reach the highest expression in his work and retain his freshness, vigor, and enthusiasm to the last, must lead a regular life.

The moment there is a falling off in the ideal, or any letting down of standards, a decline in physical or mental force, the deterioration expresses itself at once in everything one does.

Every day's work should be a supreme event in every life. We should come to it as carefully prepared as the *prima donna*, who is trying to hold the world's supremacy in song, comes before her audience. Then our work would breathe out the vigor and vitality and freshness which we put into it. Then life would be glorified, and the work of the world illuminated, transformed.

XXXV.

DON'T TAKE YOUR BUSINESS TROUBLES HOME.

A JUDGE of large experience says that one of the chief grievances of women who come to him for relief through divorce is that their husbands neglect them and their homes for business, giving their minds so completely to affairs that even when at home they are only surly brutes with whom the angels themselves could not lead happy domestic lives.

We all know men who are agreeable and cheerful at the club, but who become cross and intolerably disagreeable the moment they get home. They seem to think that they have license to vent their spleen at home, as it belongs to them. If any one has injured them during the day, they seem to try to get even by maltreating members of their own family. Some men rarely look pleasant in their homes. They reserve their sunshine for the outside world; they carry their gloom, their sadness, and their melancholy home for family consumption. Their home-coming is dreaded as a disturbing element. Many a man thwarts all his wife's efforts at home-making by turning a smiling face to the world, and a sour, fault-finding one to his home.

Think of such a man coming home to snarl at a woman who loves him in spite of his faults, and who has remained home all day caring for the children, enduring the thousand and one annoyances of housekeeping and baby tending. She has been trying to make the home the cleanest, sweetest place on earth for her little ones and her husband, waiting and watching for his return, and then is grieved to the heart to have him return with a haggard, repulsive face, worn out and disgruntled because something has gone wrong in his business. He enters with a growl for his greeting, pushing the children out of the way, and taking refuge as soon as possible behind a book or a paper. Then he wonders why his home is not more agreeable, why his wife does not think more of him, and why his children do not run to meet him with the old-time joy and gladness. Some of them even complain that their homes are not congenial, and that, if they could get the home encouragement, support, and harmony that they crave, they would be more successful.

My dear friend, how much have you ever done to deserve the harmony, love, and encouragement which you fail to get? Did you ever realize what it means to the sensitive girl whom you have taken out of congenial, harmonious surroundings, and put into a strange home, to be greeted with a grunt or a growl, and met with a face full of disgust with all the world, herself seemingly included? Do you wonder that this gentle, responsive soul becomes discouraged after a while, and meets you with indifference? Do you wonder that your children, sensitive to your moods, prefer to play by themselves, or with other children, rather than to be pushed from the knees of the man who never has time to fondle them, or to romp and play with them? Do you, fathers, wonder that your daughters are not fonder of you? Why, they scarcely know you except by a hurried "Good-night," and the check that is given to pay the quarter at the boarding school. You have not taken the time to get acquainted with your family. Perhaps you have seen less of your sons and daughters in the years when they have been coming to manhood and womanhood than have their chums and friends. You may know less about them than your neighbors do.

Your children are naturally as full of play as young kittens. They do not know anything about your business troubles. When they see you come home they ought to think of you as a new playfellow, fresh from the mysterious "down-town." They cannot imagine anything more important than to have fun, — and you would not have them think otherwise. You want to keep the serious side of life from them as long as possible, to prolong their childhood, so that they may develop normally and their hearts may be tender and responsive to the noble things of life.

Oh, how many fathers crush all the spontaneous, bubbling spirit out of the lives of their children by trying to make them adults in their childhood! It is a sorry day when a child gets the impression that his father is not his playmate, or when he does not long for him to come home so that he can have a good time. He easily becomes discouraged and disheartened when he is constantly told, "Don't do that," or "Get away." His spontaneity is soon dampened and his enthusiasm quenched. He becomes prematurely sour, cynical, and pessimistic. Is there a more pitiable picture than a long, anxious face upon a child, or lines of trouble already engraved upon youthful brows, and pallor where roses ought to be? What should the expression of maturity and care have to do with childish features? What have worry and anxiety about the future to do with childhood? Fathers, you do not know what you are doing when you rob your own flesh and blood of its childish joy. It is cruelty.

If optimism were woven into the very life and fiber of a child until it reached maturity, pessimism would have very little chance with it afterwards. The ideal father and mother of the future will never allow fear, anxiety, or worry to stamp its hideous image upon a child's life, for sunshine, sweetness, beauty, cheerfulness, and love will dominate the future home so completely that there will be no chance for shadows, discord, and a thousand other enemies of happiness to do their deadly work.

Ah! complaining man, the joys of the home come from giving and taking; they cannot be all one-sided. You cannot expect your wife and children to run with joy to meet such a crabbed, cross, disgruntled, forbidding creature as you are every night. Human nature is not made on that plan. Suppose you should go home and find your wife and home presenting such a forbidding, dejected, discouraging picture as you present! How would you like, every night, on your arrival at home, to have your wife fill your ears with all the little troubles she has had during the day with the servants and the hundreds of little annoyances that come to every housekeeper? You would not go home at all to such a greeting, if you could help it. A model wife and mother hides these unpleasant things from her husband. She knows that he does not wish to be bothered or annoyed with them. She is determined to meet him with a cheerful face and a smile, so that his home may seem the pleasantest place on earth to him. You must bring sunshine with you if you expect it to be reflected back to you. You cannot expect to get sunshine in return for gloom, despondency, irritability, and crabbedness. The rate of exchange is not that way. Your home is an investment, and you will get back in kind just what you put into it, with plenty of interest. If your investment is mean, stingy, and contemptible, you cannot expect to draw large dividends of sweetness, serenity, repose, and happiness. A home is a bank of happiness. If you deposit counterfeit money, you cannot expect to draw out the genuine coin of social exchange. Home is like a whispering gallery, and the echoes must follow the initial impulse or voice. It is like a mirror which reflects whatever face you make into it. If you scowl, it will scowl back; if you laugh, it will laugh in response. There is no way for you to get happiness out of a home unless you put happiness-material into it.

Not only on account of your home, but also on your own account, you should not keep business in mind all the time. A bow that is always bent loses its elasticity, so that it will not send the arrow home with force when there is need. A man who is thinking day and night about his business weakens his faculties, and loses his buoyancy and "snap," by never allowing them a chance to become freshened, strengthened, and rejuvenated. He becomes narrow and selfish; his sympathies and affections become atrophied or petrified. Home recreation broadens a man, enlarges his sympathies, and exercises many faculties that necessarily lie dormant during the stress of business hours.

If you will make a practice, in your leisure hours, of giving yourself up completely to recreation, to having a grand, good romp with the children, or a social game with the whole family, making up your mind that you will have a good time during the evening, no matter what may happen on the morrow, you will find yourself in much better condition the next day to enter the business or professional arena. You will be much fresher and stronger, will have much more elasticity and spontaneity, and will do your work much easier, and with much less friction, than if you think, think, think of business all the time you are at home.

No matter if your business affairs are not going just as you would have them, you are only wasting the energy and mental power which would enable you to overcome these unfortunate conditions by dragging your business into your home, and worrying and fretting your family about things that they cannot help.

If you would form the habit of locking all your cross-grained, crabbed, ugly, critical nagging and worrying in your store or office at night, and resolve that, whether your business or profession is a success or a failure, your home shall be a success, — the happiest, sweetest, and cleanest place on earth to you and yours, you would find it a greater investment than any you ever made in a business way.

It is a reflection upon your own business ability that you cannot make a living during business hours. Your ill humor is a confession to your wife of your weakness and incapacity, and of your not being master of the situation, or equal to confronting emergencies. Women naturally admire strength, capacity, efficiency, and courage in men. They admire a man who cannot only make a living, but also make it easily, without fretting, stewing, or worrying. Your wife will think less of you if you continually lug home your business cares.

This does not mean that you should not keep your wife informed about your business. Every man should talk over his affairs with his wife, and she should always know the exact condition of his business. Many a man has come to grief by keeping his wife in ignorance of his straitened circumstances or declining business, or of the fact that he was temporarily pressed for capital and unable to indulge in certain luxuries. A good wife will help a man amazingly in his business troubles or struggles to get established if she knows just how he is situated and what is required of her. Her economy and her planning may give just the needed support; her sympathy may take out the sting of the pain, and enable him to bear his trials. This confiding frankly in a wife is a very different thing from everlastingly harping on the disagreeable features of a business or letting them ruin your attitude toward your family, making life miserable for those not to blame.

Good cheer, a feeling of good-will toward one another and toward other people, and a spirit of helpfulness and utter unselfishness should always be present in the home. It should be regarded as the most sacred spot on earth. The husband should look upon it as the one place in all the world where he can get away from business troubles, and the exactions, grinding, and crowding of life's struggles, — a place to which he can flee from all inharmony and discord, and find peace and rest, contentment and satisfaction. It should be a place where he always longs to go, and from which he is loath to part.

Better fail in money-making than in home-making.

XXXVI.

DO YOU KNOW ENOUGH TO KEEP YOUNG?

AGE will never succeed in retaining a youthful appearance and mentality until people make up their minds not to let the years count, — until they cease to make the body old by the constant suggestions of the mind. We begin to sow the seed-thoughts of age in youth. We look forward to being old at forty-five, and to going down hill at fifty.

The very act of preparing for old age hastens it. As Job said, "The thing I feared most has come upon me." People who prepare for a thing and look for it, anticipating, fearing, dreading it in their daily lives, usually get it.

There is a great deal in the association of ideas. Never for a moment allow yourself to think that you are too old to do this or that, for your thoughts and convictions will very soon outpicture themselves in a wrinkled face and a prematurely old expression. There is nothing better established than the philosophy that we are what we think, and that we become like our thoughts.

Never smother the impulse to act in a youthful manner because you think you are too old. Recently, at a family gathering, the boys were trying to get their father, past sixty, to play with them. " Oh, go away, go away!" he said; "I am too old for that." But the mother entered into their sports, apparently with just as much enthusiasm and real delight as if she were only their age. The youthful spirit shone in her eyes and manifested itself in every movement. Her frolic with the boys explains why she looks so much younger than her husband, in spite of the very slight difference in their years.

Be always as young as you feel, and keep young by associating with young people and taking an interest in their interests, hopes, plans, and amusements. The vitality of youth is contagious.

When questioned as to the secret of his marvelous youthfulness, in his eightieth year, Oliver Wendell Holmes replied that it was due chiefly "to a cheerful disposition and invariable contentment in every period of my life with what I was. I never felt the pangs of ambition. . . . It is restlessness, ambition, discontent and disquietude that makes us grow old prematurely by carving wrinkles on our faces. Wrinkles do not appear on faces that have constantly smiled. Smiling is the best possible massage. Contentment is the fountain of youth."

We need to practise the contentment extolled by the genial doctor, which is not the contentment of inertness, but the freeing ourselves from entangling vanities, petty cares, worries, and anxieties, which hamper us in our real life-work. The sort of ambition he condemns is that in which egotism and vanity figure most conspicuously, and in which notoriety, the praise and admiration of the world, wealth, and personal aggrandizement are the objects sought, rather than the power to be of use in the world, to be a leader in the service of humanity, and

OLIVER WENDELL HOLMES.

to be the noblest, best, and most efficient worker that one can be. It is the useless complexities in which vanity and unworthy ambition entangle us that wear away life and make so many Americans old men and women at forty. The simple life can be the fullest, noblest, and most useful.

If you would live long, love your work and continue doing it. Don't lay it down at fifty, because you think your powers are on the wane, or that you need a rest. Take a vacation whenever you require it, but don't give up your work. There is life,— there is youth in it. " I cannot grow old," says a noted actress, " because I love my art. I spend my life absorbed in it. I am never bored. How can one have lines of age or weariness or discontent when one is happy, busy, never fatigued, and one's spirit is ever, ever young? When I am tired it is not my soul, but just my body."

"We do not count a man's years," said Emerson, " until he has nothing else to count." It is not the years that age us so much as the use we make of them, and the way we live them. Excesses of any kind are fatal to longevity or the prolongation of youth.

Bitter memories of a sinful life which has gone all wrong make premature furrows in the face, take the brightness from the eyes and the elasticity from the step and make one's life sapless and uninteresting.

The Bible teaches that a clean life, a pure life, a simple life, and a useful life shall be long. " His flesh shall be fresher than a child's. He shall return to the days of his youth."

We grow old because we do not know enough to keep young, just as we become sick and diseased because we do not know enough to keep well. Sickness is a result of ignorance and wrong thinking. The time will come when a man will no more harbor thoughts that will make him sick or weak than he would think of putting his hands into fire. No man can be sick if he always has right thoughts and takes ordinary care of his body. If he will think only youthful thoughts he can maintain his youth far beyond the usual period.

If you would "be young when old" adopt the sun dial's motto — "I record none but hours of sunshine." Never mind the dark or shadowed hours. Forget the unpleasant, unhappy days. Remember only the days of rich experience; let the others drop into oblivion.

It is said that "long livers are great hopers." If you keep your hope bright in spite of discouragements, and meet all difficulties with a cheerful face, it will be very difficult for age to trace its furrows on your brow. There is longevity in cheerfulness.

Don't let go love or love of romance; they are amulets against wrinkles. If the mind is constantly bathed in love, and filled with helpful, charitable sentiments toward all, the body will keep fresh and vigorous many years longer than it will if the heart is dried up and emptied of human sympathy by a selfish, greedy life. The heart that is kept warm by love is never frozen by age or chilled by prejudice, fear, or anxious thought. A French beauty used to have herself massaged with mutton tallow every night, in order to keep her muscles elastic and her body supple. A better way of preserving youthful elasticity is coming into vogue — massaging the mind with love thoughts, beauty thoughts, cheerful thoughts, and young ideals.

If you do not want the years to count, look forward instead of backward, and put as much variety and as many interests into your life as possible. Monotony and lack of mental occupation are great age-producers. Women who live in cities, in the midst of many interests and great variety, preserve their youth and good looks, as a rule, much longer than women who live in remote country places, who get no variety into their lives, and who have no interests outside their narrow daily round of monotonous duties, which require no exercise of the mind. Insanity is an alarmingly increasing result of the monotony of women's lives on the farm. It is worth noting, too, that farmers who live so much outdoors, and in an environment much more healthful than that of the average brain-worker, do not live so long as the latter.

When Solon, the Athenian sage, was asked the secret of his strength and youth, he replied that it was "learning something new every day." This belief was general among the ancient Greeks — that the secret of eternal youth is "to be always learning something new."

There is the basis of a great truth in the idea. It is healthful activity that strengthens and preserves the mind as well as the body, and gives it youthful quickness and elasticity. So, if you would be young, in spite of the years, you must remain receptive to new thought, and must grow broader in spirit, wider in sympathy, and more and more open to fresh revelations of truth as you travel farther on the road of life.

But the greatest conqueror of age is a cheerful, hopeful, loving spirit. A man who would conquer the years must have charity for all. He must avoid worry, envy, malice, and jealousy — all the small meannesses that feed bitterness in the heart, trace wrinkles on the brow, and dim the eye. A pure heart, a sound body, and a broad, healthy, generous mind, backed by a determination not to let the years count, constitute a fountain of youth which every one may find in himself.

XXXVII.

LET IT GO.

Do not hang on to the things that keep you back, that make you unhappy. Let go of the worry; let go of the anxiety; let go of the scolding, fretting, and fuming; let go of criticism; let go of fear; let go of the anxious, over-strenuous life; let go of selfish living; let go of the rubbish, the useless, the foolish, the silly; let go of the shams, the shoddy, the false; let go the straining to keep up appearances; let go of the superficial; let go of the vice that cripples, the false thinking that demoralizes; and you will be surprised to see how much lighter and freer and truer you are to run the race, and how much surer of the goal.

If you have had an unfortunate experience, forget it. If you have made a failure in speech, your song, your book, your article, if you have been placed in an embarrassing position, if you have fallen and hurt yourself by a false step, if you have been slandered and abused, do not dwell upon it. There is not a single redeeming feature in these memories, and the presence of their ghosts will rob you of many a happy hour. There is nothing in it. Drop them. Forget them. Wipe them out of your mind forever. If you have been indiscreet, imprudent, if you have been talked about, if your reputation has been injured so that you fear you can never outgrow it or redeem it, do not drag the hideous shadows, the rattling skeletons about with you. Rub them off from the slate of memory. Wipe them out. Forget them. Start with a clean slate and spend all your energies in keeping it clean for the future.

Resolve that whatever you do or do not do, you will not be haunted by skeletons, that you will not cherish shadows. They must get out and give place to the sunshine. Determine that you will have nothing to do with discords, that every one of them must get out of your mind. No matter how formidable or persistent, wipe them out. Forget them. Have nothing to do with them. Do not let the little enemies — worrying and foreboding, anxiety and regrets — sap your energy, for this is your capital for future achievement.

A gloomy face, a sour expression, a worrying mind, a fretting disposition, are proofs of your failure to control yourself. They are the earmarks of your weakness, a confession of your inability to cope with your environment. Drive them away. Scatter them to the four winds. Dominate yourself. Do not let your enemies sit on the throne. Do your own governing.

"Dismiss from your mind every suggestion that has to do with illness. If you have had an operation, — it is over, let it glide into the shadows, the background of memory. Do not dwell upon it, do not talk about it."

Whatever is disagreeable, whatever irritates, nags, destroys your balance of mind, forget it — thrust it out. It has nothing to do with you now. You have better use for your time than to waste it in regrets in worry, in useless trifles. Let go the rubbish. Make war upon despondency, if you are subject to it. Drive the blues out of your mind as you would a thief out of the house.

Shut the door in the face of all your enemies, and keep it shut. Do not wait for cheerfulness to come to you. Go after it; entertain it; never let it go.

A despondent young writer says that while he was in the West he used to watch the cows on the prairies and he could not help envying them. "I used often to heave a sigh and wish I were a cow." "What keeps them so contented?" he asked the farmer. "Oh, they are enjoying themselves chewing the cud," was the reply.

The trouble with many of us is, we do not enjoy chewing the cud, — letting go of the aches and pains, the anxieties, and just enjoying ourselves. We cannot bear to let go. We cling like a thrifty housewife, who cannot bear to throw away a rag or a scrap of anything, but piles the useless rubbish in the attic. We cannot bear to let go of our enemies. We cannot seem to kick out of doors the things that worry and fret and chafe, and yet never do us any good.

The American people do not know how to let go. We keep our muscles tense and nerves up to such a pitch that it is the hardest thing in the world for us to drop things. We chafe and worry and fret instead of just resting without being haunted by the skeletons of care, of anxiety, and of business.

Who can estimate the medicinal power of one cheerful life in the home, — of one serene, balanced soul?

"My young partners do the work and I do the laughing, and I commend to you the thought that there is very little success where there is little laughter," says Andrew Carnegie. The workman who rejoices in his work and laughs away his discomfort is the man who is sure to rise, for it is what we do easily and what we like to do that we do well.

The most of us make our backs ache carrying useless, foolish burdens. We carry luggage and rubbish that are of no earthly use, but which sap our strength and keep us jaded and tired to no purpose. If we could only learn to hold on to the things worth while, and drop the rubbish, — let go the useless, the foolish, the silly, the hamperers, the things that hinder, — we should not only make progress but we should keep happy and harmonious.

XXXVIII.

THE ROLL CALL OF THE GREAT.

IF the roll were called for the truly great, who would dare to answer? Would it be those who have clean hearts and clean hands, who have taken advantage of no one, but have helped everybody, and have retarded no one's progress; would it be those whose lives have been a perpetual benediction of cheerfulness, encouragement, helpfulness, and inspiration, regardless of whether they have accumulated money or not; or would it be those who have blocked the way for others and used them as stepping-stones upon which to climb to their own goal, regardless of their welfare; would it be those who figure most conspicuously in the gaze of the world and the publicity of newspapers?

If the roll were called, and only really honest responses were accepted, would not thousands of so-called successful men of wealth be dumb? Would not many who figure in the world's fame also be mute? Would not the tongue of a man be tied whose success is full of the ghosts of ruined lives?

When will the world learn that heart-wealth is the only real wealth, that money in itself is contemptible in comparison with noble deeds? When shall we learn that the accumulation of money often represents the lowest human faculties, the coarser side of man in which the finer instincts have no part? Grasping, seizing, piling one dollar on another is not success.

Who can estimate what the world owes to those who, according to the ordinary modern standard of success, have failed? Who can compute the debt of civilization to the men and women who in their efforts to make the world a little brighter, a little better place in which to live, have been too busy to make money?

When the genius of history unrolls the scroll of earth's benefactors, it will be found that many of those who stand highest on the list were hardly recognized during their lives. The name of many a servant will be above that of his master. Many a humble employee will be found to have been, in reality, more successful than the proprietor of the establishment in which he worked. The name of many a day-laborer, whose life was absorbed in making a modest home comfortable, and in trying to give his children a better education, a better start in life than he had, will be found written far above those of men who were lauded in print, and were looked up to as eminently successful.

It will be easy to find the story of some boy who remained on the farm and helped to pay the mortgage, stifled his ambition in order that the favorite brother might be sent to college, and thereby scored a much greater success than the one for whom the sacrifice was made.

The girl who smothered her longings for a higher education, or sacrificed the prospects of marriage and a home of her own, in order to take care of her aged parents, and was not known outside of her little coterie of friends, may have her name recorded far higher on the honor roll than that of the sister who went to college, or became a great author, musician, artist, or actress.

Not a few employers will be surprised to find the names of those who have made their wealth possible — those whose ambitions they have crushed, whose hopes they have blasted, whose opportunities they have cramped, and to whom they have never given a kind or encouraging word — emblazoned in shining characters in that list of chosen ones where they will look in vain for their own.

Many a mill-owner will be amazed to find the names of his poor operatives, who worked in the unhealthy, gloomy mill, early and late, year in and year out, and whom he never recognized, — emaciated boys and girls, compelled by an unfortunate economic system to work when they should have been at school, bent and feeble fathers and mothers, and little children, who never knew the joys of childhood, — standing out accusingly, while his own and those of his pampered children are nowhere visible.

The arrogant millionaire will be likely to find, far above his own, the names of his coachman, housemaid, and cook, — so-called menials, — on whom, perhaps, he and his family looked as beings of an inferior world.

Many a successful merchant will look in vain for the name of an idolized and over-indulged son, but will find that of a despised office boy, an unnoticed clerk, or an overworked and under-paid stenographer.

No one will live long in the world's memory, or find a place on the honor roll, who has not done something besides selfishly grasping and holding the "almighty dollar," or working within the narrow sphere of personal interests and ambitions.

Achievement is not always success, while reputed failure often is. It is honest endeavor, persistent effort to do the best possible under any and all circumstances, daily practice of the Golden Rule, scattering little deeds of love and kindness along life's pathway, and aspiration to be of use in the world, that will win a place in the ranks of the elect.

Fame, wealth, position, worldly honors, — these have nothing to do with real success. The most successful Man that ever lived was despised of men, and so poor that He had not where to lay His head.

Ah, how shrunken and pitiful a thing, what a delusion, is the so-called success of self-absorbed men and women!

They who trample under foot every sentiment of human pity, love, and kindness, who brush aside opportunities to help brighten other lives as so many obstacles to the achievement of their ambition, — whatever it may be, — will cut sorry figures when their accounts are balanced. Like that private soldier into whose hands there fell, when Galerius sacked the camp of the Persians, "a bag of shining leather filled with pearls," and who, according to Gibbon, the historian, "carefully preserved the bag, but threw away the contents," they will find that they have spurned true riches, real success, to grasp what is false.

In the white light of history, before the tribunal of justice, we shall not be judged for what we seem to be or have achieved, but for what we are and by what we have tried to do.

In the judgment of this tribunal, from which there is no appeal, many failures will be approved as successes, and many successes will be adjudged failures.

In imperishable characters, there will be inscribed on the success roll of honor names unfamiliar to most of us, the names of those who nobly performed humble parts in life: the unknown workers for humanity, the heroic sufferers, — some blind, some crippled or handicapped by the loss of hands or feet, or tortured by incurable disease, — who, with a fortitude equal to that of the martyrs of old, took up life's burdens and bravely made the most of the powers and opportunities bestowed upon them by the Almighty.

Ingram Content Group UK Ltd.
Milton Keynes UK
UKHW011059060723
424663UK00002B/28

9 781528 713948

The Cinderella Prince

HAYDEN HALL